# STUDY  SKILLS

# THE
# WORLD
# BOOK

## Volume
# 1

# STUDY SKILLS

Published by
**World Book, Inc.**
a Scott Fetzer company
Chicago

# Staff

**Publisher**
William H. Nault

**Editorial**

**Editor in Chief**
Robert O. Zeleny

**Executive Editor**
Dominic J. Miccolis

**Associate Editor**
Maureen M. Mostyn

**Senior Editor**
Michael K. Urban

**Writers**
Marjorie Eberts
Margaret Gisler

**Production Editor**
Elizabeth Ireland

**Index Editor**
Joyce Goldenstern

**Permissions Editor**
Janet T. Peterson

**Editorial Assistant**
Elizabeth Lepkowski

**Art**

**Executive Art Director**
William Hammond

**Designers**
Tessing Design, Inc.

**Production Artist**
Cynthia Schultz

**Photography Director**
John S. Marshall

**Photographers**
Don Sala
Jim Ballard

**Product Production**

**Executive Director**
Peter Mollman

**Manufacturing**
Joseph C. La Count, director

**Research and Development**
Henry Koval, manager

**Pre-Press Services**
Jerry Stack, director
Randi Park
Sandra Van den Broucke

**Proofreaders**
Marguerite Hoye, head
Ann Dillon
Esther Johns
Daniel Marotta

Copyright © 1986 by
World Book, Inc.
Merchandise Mart Plaza
Chicago, Illinois 60654

Printed in the United States of America

ISBN 0-7166-3185-7 (Volume 1)
ISBN 0-7166-3184-9 (set)
Library of Congress Catalog No. 86-50558
b/hf

# Contents

# Introduction

Your study habits play a crucial role in determining your success in school. If your study habits are good, you should have little trouble getting good grades in your classes. But if you have poor study habits, you will be constantly struggling through your schoolwork. *Study Skills* presents proper study habits and explains how to organize and make the most of your study time.

The first section, "Why You Should Study," stresses the importance of studying, and it helps you assess your current study habits. The next two sections teach you how to set up a study area and how to make a study schedule and stick to it.

Section IV is entitled "Study Aids," and it describes many different items in your home and at school that can be helpful when you are studying. The fifth section, "The Best Way to Study," explains how to make outlines, underline important material, and take notes. It also explains how to use the SQ3R study method, and it gives special methods of study for major subject areas. The final section tells you who to turn to for special help with your study problems.

The further you go in your educational career, the more studying you will be required to do. Use this volume to help you develop the study habits you need in order to succeed now and in the future.

# I WHY YOU SHOULD STUDY

*This section tells you why studying is an important lifelong activity. Your current study habits will also be assessed.*

# New England Colonies

What were the thirteen original colonies?

What was the Massachusetts Bay Colony?

What were the Puritans?

en ships
omen, and
to New Eng-
year, more ships
l there were 2,000
ew World. They called
**Massachusetts Bay**
he biggest town in that
was named **Boston.** Later, Ply-
would become a part of the
ony, and the colony would be called
simply **Massachusetts.**

Many of the Puritans were wealthier
han their neighbors in Plymouth. Mas-
usetts quickly became a prosperous
f trade and commerce. *Boston*
*one of the most important*
ica.

69

# Why You Should Study

From the day you walked into your first classroom, you have been studying. Just try to imagine the number of hours that you have already spent preparing for tests, completing your homework, reading textbooks, taking notes, making outlines, and memorizing dates. It is mind boggling. Now seems like a very good time to make sure that you are studying efficiently and effectively, especially since you still have several years of schooling to complete. Study becomes increasingly important as you move from elementary school to high school and then on to college. Besides, you will find that studying does not end when you leave school. To keep up in this modern technological age, you must study throughout your life.

The word *studying* turns off many students by bringing up thoughts of being locked in a quiet room, nose buried in a book, frantically trying to memorize facts that do not seem very important. Many students do not realize that studying is not necessarily limited to textbooks. Science can be studied by walking in the woods to observe plants, by cutting up frogs in the science lab, or by looking at the stars through a telescope. English can be studied by taking part in plays, seeing classic movies, or watching plays on television. Mathematics can be studied by using flashcards, playing dominoes, or using a calculator. Social studies can be studied by reading newspapers and magazines or by listening to the news on television. Foreign languages, history, and geography can all be studied by traveling to different parts of the country or other parts of the world.

Studying, of course, is not limited to school subjects. You are studying when you learn how to develop photographic negatives by reading a book or watching the techniques of a friend who knows how to develop negatives. You are studying when someone shows you how to make an omelet or change the oil filter in a car. When you are practicing in the gym, you could be studying the skill of throwing a basketball through a hoop, doing a backwards somersault on a balance beam, or serving a volleyball. You can study by reading, observing, listening, or doing. Studying is your effort to learn about any subject. It is an activity that allows you to obtain information, acquire greater understanding, or improve a skill.

## Why Study?

There is really no single answer to the question "Why study?" Everyone has different reasons for studying. Obviously, for most students the answer is to succeed in school. You will use some of this learning right away. And some of this learning you will need to store away for the future. For example, you must study mathematics so that you have number skills for immediate use, such as doing your math homework or passing tests. Yet such mathematical skills as counting money, balancing checkbooks, paying bills, and filing income tax returns are required of just about everyone throughout their lives. You are studying English now so that you can write term papers, compositions, and reports. Later on, you will use this knowledge to write résumés, to fill in job and college applications, and to appreciate good literature.

Right now, you may have blinders on and may not be able to find any reason to study except to pass the test this Friday. But it won't be long before you are using what once seemed like worthless information just to get by in this increasingly complex world.

## The World Is Changing

Long ago, a person who had mastered the skills and knowledge essential to an occupation was set for life. For example, it did not take farmers very long to teach their children everything that they would need to know to run their own farms. Adding little, the children could pass that knowledge on in an equally short period of time to their children and so on down through generations.

This is no longer the case. To be a successful farmer today, a person must know so much that it may require a college education to master the needed skills and technology. Just to grow a crop like wheat, a farmer must know enough about chemistry to choose the appropriate fertilizers for the different kinds of soil on the farm and to decide what kind of weedkillers will work best. Many farmers today use computers in the operation of their farms.

## Don't Be Left Behind

*Mastering study skills in school is not only a means for current success. It is fast becoming a ticket to survival in the future.*

Rapid change has affected so many occupations that the person who does not keep up might end up washed out of a job. Newly developed office machinery forces typists to become word processors, a position that requires new skills and knowledge. Doctors, dentists, and engineers—among others—can scarcely keep up with new knowledge that almost daily affects their fields.

For example, what a mechanic in the 1920's learned about the Model-T Ford is of little use today. The mechanic's skill in repairing a Model-T Ford would not help to repair a modern, eight-cylinder, high-powered engine. Not only is the engine itself a more complicated mechanism, but so are the tools needed to repair it. A mechanic today must be able to study a car manual and be able to translate the procedures and ideas on the printed page into action in the garage. And what about the cars of the future? Will there be atomic-powered cars? Will cars be powered by electricity?

Whether the task is to keep up with an occupation or to learn a new one, the only way to survive is to study. And by the time one is finished with formal schooling, it is rather late in the day to learn how. Mastering study skills in school, and the sooner the better, is not only a means for current success. It is fast becoming a ticket to survival in the future. Culture and technology are advancing so rapidly that many people are now faced with the danger of being left behind.

## What About the Future?

There is yet another consideration. Seldom, if ever, does a person have only one occupational goal in life. There are very few people today who are not involved in a hobby of some sort or who do not pursue any one of a number of part-time interests. In addition to following an occupation, you might also wish to become an accomplished golfer, or a bridge or poker player, or a member of an amateur photo or chess club. Of course, sharpening your off-the-job and after-school skills is not always a chore; it is usually a pleasant activity. Even so, success at a hobby or part-time activity requires that you have the ability to study efficiently.

It is important that you learn how to learn, or learn how to study. You will find you need continuous study to meet the challenges of the future. Schools cannot do the whole job of educating. Schools do not have enough time. You will have to continue learning and studying long after you have left school.

## Role of the Student

Today, the educational system is full of people who are eager to help you learn. However, you and you alone must accept most of the responsibility for your learning. You must arrive at school on time, complete your assignments, pay attention in class, do your homework, and pass tests. You must also study efficiently for each and every one of your classes. All of this requires both discipline and commitment. Students often feel that these are qualities that they will acquire and apply once they have a job. What is important for you to understand is that you already have a job—that of student. The work habits and attitudes toward responsibility that you develop in school will be the ones you carry over to your first job.

It is easy to take full responsibility for getting A's. However, how much responsibility do you take for an occasional D or F? Have you ever excused poor grades by making remarks like:

> "My mother didn't have time to check my book report this morning."

> "Who needs this class anyway?"

> "The teacher expects too much from me."

> "The basketball game got over too late last night for me to study."

> "Mary told me it was not worth my time to read the book."

*If you don't believe in yourself and your ability to succeed at school, you need to reprogram your thinking.*

The students who feel most satisfied with their study efforts are the ones who take full credit for their failures as well as their successes. Not only do they say, "I studied the spelling words every night this week so I could win the spelling bee," but they also say, "It's my fault for not passing the math test. I watched too much television last night."

## Think Positively

No one who has won an Olympic gold medal ever said, "I'm not really a very good athlete," or "I'll never be good enough to win a medal." Whether they are Olympic athletes or successful students, winners share a common attitude—they believe in themselves. They seem to have little voices in their heads that always say, "I can succeed. I will succeed." A positive attitude will help you face impossible teachers, difficult tests, tedious homework, and strict grading systems. If you don't believe in yourself and your ability to succeed at school, you need to reprogram your thinking now.

### *Check Your Attitude*

Take a few minutes to find out if you have negative attitudes about school that may be affecting your work. Copy the following list on a piece of paper. Put a check by each statement that describes your attitude toward school:

1. _____ My teachers don't like me.

2. _____ Studying has little effect on the grades I get.

3. _____ The teaching in my school is not very good.

4. _____ I never get any credit for trying.

5. _____ It is just luck if I ever get an A.

6. _____ It is not important to pay attention in class.

7. _____ Doing homework is a waste of time.

8. _____ It is not essential to hand in neat work.

9. _____ Eating good food and getting plenty of rest do not help students do better work.

10. _____ A good attendance record is not necessary.

11. _____ What I am learning in school is not related to my career plans.

12. _____ Having a regular study time is not necessary.

13. _____ An assignment notebook is a waste of paper.

14. _____ Textbooks bore me to death.

15. _____ Grades aren't important.

## Change Your Attitude

Count the number of checks you have made. If you have five or more checks, your attitude toward school is too negative and is probably keeping you from being success-ful. Fortunately, attitudes are habits, and habits can be changed.

Start by eliminating negative words like "can't," "never," and "impossible" from your vocabulary. Get in the habit of saying positive things to yourself like:

"If I pay more attention in class, my homework will be easier."

"If I take time every night to organize myself, the day will go better at school."

"If I do my homework regularly, my grades will im-prove."

## Get Interested in Studying

Part of the secret to acquiring a positive attitude toward school is developing a genuine interest in studying. It is up to you to develop this interest. No one—parents, teachers, counselors, or friends—can do it for you. You can't possibly expect to be interested in studying every subject. You may be interested in math and find it fascinating to reduce fractions or do long division. Your best friend may find it an absolute bore to study math, but he or she may love to study English. However, if you begin to put in a serious effort to study a subject that you do not find particularly interesting, you will begin to have some success with that subject and be more willing to study it since you see your efforts paying off.

## Motivate Yourself

*When you are self-motivated, you have taken a giant step toward becoming a successful student.*

Once you have developed a genuine interest in a subject, you will find that you are increasingly motivated to study it. When you are self-motivated, you have taken a giant step toward becoming a successful student. However, with all the distractions around you, it is not always easy to start a study session. Studying isn't very appealing when you could be talking with your friends on the telephone, watching a favorite program on television, listening to your radio, or settling down with a big bowl of popcorn to see the latest video. And your study sessions also have to compete with lots of very interesting activities like cheerleading, football games, school plays, club meetings, dances, and parties.

If your social activities do not compete with your study time, there are always other things that bite into this time. Many students have to spend time every day working at their jobs, practicing music or a sport, or babysitting a younger brother or sister. Nor can you forget the thousands of other things that compete for your study time, such as doctor's appointments, haircuts, shopping, and even visiting your grandparents.

You have to be strongly motivated in order to be able to turn your back on social activities that lure you from your study time. Often you must turn down an invitation so that you can type a term paper, finish your homework, begin a science fair project, or study for a quiz. It is also up to you to make the decision about how you are going to spend your time. You will probably have to give up some activities in order to spend sufficient time studying.

To be adequately motivated to study, you must set goals for yourself. Without goals to give you direction, you will find that you are making lots of little decisions each day about whether or not to study, where to study, and even how to study. And you will frequently decide against studying because the other activities are more attractive. A student without goals travels around with no more direction than a paper airplane in the wind.

## Setting Goals

Every person has goals that he or she would like to reach. People who set moderate goals that can be achieved with a small amount of effort quickly build up their self-confidence. And then they can go on to set more difficult goals. As you work toward achieving your goals, you need to have rewards built in. For example, after doing a very difficult math homework assignment or reading a boring story for English, you might want to take time for your favorite snack. When you know that there is a reward, it makes you stick to a task. A reward is anything that is important to you. It could be food, a break, a pat on the back from your family or teacher, or watching a TV show.

## Immediate Goals

Take the time right now to begin setting up some immediate goals that you want to achieve in your studying. Be sure to choose only those goals that you can reach quickly. If there is too long a time lag before you can achieve a goal, you may well find yourself getting discouraged.

## The First Step

Consider your present situation. Are you barely passing math? Could you easily change your C in science to a B? With a little effort, could you learn all the dates for the next history test? Your first goals should be survival goals—goals that will help you keep afloat in the classroom. Be realistic as you make these goals. Set ones that you can quickly achieve within a few days or at the most a week.

*Your first goals should be survival goals—goals that will help you keep afloat in the classroom.*

Don't set too many goals. It is admirable to have the goals of reading a five-hundred-page book for English, getting an A on the math quiz, winning a place on the debate team, making a fantastic map for social studies, and raising your typing speed by five words per minute. But don't choose to reach all these goals at the same time or you will be disappointed and reluctant to set new goals. Setting one or possibly two simple goals should get you off to a good start in improving your study habits. If you can't decide what your study goals should be, ask one of your teachers or a counselor to help you.

Write down the names of one or two subjects in which you would like to see some immediate improvement. Set one goal that you would like to reach in each course this week. You might make a chart like the one below:

| Subject | Immediate Goal |
|---|---|
| 1. English | To do my home-work every day. |
| 2. Science | To learn the parts of the atom. |

## The Second Step

Once you have written down your goals, make a list of all the materials that you will need to carry out your first goal. Then make another list of all the things that you will have to do in order to achieve that goal. Your lists for the first goal might look something like these:

## Materials

1. English textbook.
2. Paper, erasable pen, and pencil.
3. Dictionary and thesaurus.
4. Folder for English papers.
5. Assignment pad.

## Things to Do

1. I need to write down the homework assignments before I leave class each day.
2. I must remember to take my English book and folder home every night.
3. I will start my English homework by five o'clock and finish it before dinner.
4. I will ask my older brother to check my homework every night right after dinner.

Make similar lists for your second goal. Then think of ways that you are going to reward yourself. You know yourself best. Only you can decide whether you can wait to receive your reward when you reach your goal or whether you are going to need to reward yourself for each step of progress you make.

## *The Final Step*

Once you have completed your lists, you need to decide when you are going to check on your progress. For example, if you have chosen the goal of doing your homework in English, you might want to evaluate your progress in two or three days. This lets you make any necessary adjustments in implementing your goal. After you reach a goal, you should always ask yourself if you chose the best plan of action.

*After you reach a goal, you should always ask yourself if you chose the best plan of action.*

## Future Goals

Once you have achieved several immediate goals, you are ready to consider making a few long-range goals. These goals could include anything from making the honor roll this semester to thinking about what courses you might like to be studying four, six, or eight years from now. Whether a goal can be reached in a week or a year, you need to go through the same steps in order to reach that goal.

*For long-range goals, you need to set up many checkpoints along the way to help you stay on track.*

For long-range goals, you need to set up many checkpoints along the way to help you stay on track. In fact, you should probably make some kind of check list to record your progress. This would include the tasks that you need to do, the projected date of completion, and the actual date of completion. It is also a good idea to write down the reward you will receive if you complete each task on time. A student who wanted to do a science fair project on the effect of different kinds of music on plant growth made this check list:

| Tasks to Be Done | To Be Completed by | Date Completed | Reward |
| --- | --- | --- | --- |
| 1. Read guidelines for the project | Jan. 10 | Jan. 8 | ½ hour TV |
| 2. Select the project | Jan. 15 | Jan. 16 | Visit friend |
| 3. State the purpose | Jan. 20 | Jan. 19 | Candy bar |
| 4. Research the project | Jan. 28 | Jan. 30 | Movie |
| 5. Write the hypothesis | Jan. 30 | Jan. 30 | Popcorn |
| 6. Gather materials | Feb. 1 | Feb. 2 | Pizza |
| 7. Do the experiment | Feb. 4 | Feb. 7 | 2 hours TV |
| 8. List the results | Feb. 8 | Feb. 8 | Visit friend |

| | | | |
|---|---|---|---|
| 9. Draw conclusions | Feb. 9 | Feb. 9 | Ride bike |
| 10. Write the report | Feb. 12 | Feb. 12 | Video |
| 11. Prepare exhibit | Feb. 15 | Feb. 16 | T-shirt |
| 12. Prepare speech for the judges | Feb. 16 | Feb. 16 | ½ hour TV |
| 13. Attend the fair | Feb. 20 | Feb. 20 | Fast-food dinner |

Once you have acquired the habit of setting study goals and making check lists, you will find that your studying has direction. But perhaps even more important, as you begin to accomplish your first simple goals, your faith in your ability to learn will increase. And you will soon find yourself motivated to set and reach more difficult goals. There is no better way to interest yourself in studying than by setting goals. Most students should concentrate on setting goals that can be realized within a short period of time, perhaps a week. And it is best to work on reaching only a few goals at a time.

## How Well Do You Study?

Surveys of junior high school students usually show that many feel they have to do too much studying outside of school. Many students believe the kind of homework they are given is not interesting or challenging. Although they seem to find time for parties, dates, television, and sports, students never seem to have enough time for homework. They are usually behind with their notebooks, special reports, and daily lesson assignments.

However, some students who have just as many outside interests and no greater mental ability are able to keep up with their assignments. The difference is usually a matter of study habits. The reason you study in a certain way is because you have always done it that way. You are acting automatically rather than deciding how you should study.

No matter what goals you set for yourself or how interested you are in your studies, you will not meet with success in your studying unless you have good study habits.

## Checking Your Study Habits

You probably have both good and bad study habits. Now is a good time to answer the following questions about study habits. A "no" answer may indicate a study habit deficiency that should be corrected:

1. Do you have a definite place to study in your home?
2. Do you have a definite time set aside for study every day?
3. Do you study alone?
4. Do you have a dictionary in the room in which you study?
5. Do you have the TV, radio, record player, or tape player turned off when you are studying?
6. Do you study for more than one hour at a time?
7. Do you take notes while you are studying?
8. Do you make a list of questions for the things you do not understand?
9. Do you study every night?
10. Do you have good lighting in the room in which you study?
11. Do you usually study the subject that you like best first?
12. Do you skim reading assignments before reading them thoroughly?
13. Do you review classwork on a regular basis?
14. Do you take notes during class time?
15. Do you have a notebook that is carefully organized by subject matter?

16. Do you have a weekly schedule that organizes your time for study and other activities?

17. Do you look up new words in an assignment if you don't understand what they mean?

18. Do you usually understand what you read?

19. Do your grades improve when you spend long hours studying?

20. Can you master a difficult subject if you are interested in it?

21. Do you enjoy studying?

22. Do you use a special method of study for each subject?

23. Do you listen attentively to class discussions?

24. Do you usually hand in neat, well-organized work?

## Studying Is Personal

Learning is a very individualized process. What may help one student learn may not help another. But many learning and study problems can be overcome through the application of certain techniques and disciplined work. Habits can be changed. Bad habits can be replaced by good ones. It is easier to break bad habits if you tell everyone you are going to change your habits. The more good results you see, the easier it will be to continue with your new good habits.

## On the Way to Success

By reading the first section in this book, you have demonstrated that you are interested in learning how to study. Quite clearly, you want to acquire study techniques that will help you achieve success at school. You have accepted the responsibility for your learning. Hopefully, you have begun to acquire the habit of thinking positively about yourself. As soon as you reach one of the goals that you set for yourself earlier in this section, you will have definite proof that you can become a better student.

# II THE BEST PLACE TO STUDY

*Where you study is just as important as how you study. This section helps you set up the proper environment for study.*

THE WORLD ALMANAC

INTERNATIONAL Thesaurus

FOURTH EDITION

World Book ATLAS of the United States and Canada

WORLD BOOK DICTIONARY

The Mineral Kingdom

A-K

CROWELL

# The Best Place to Study

*S*tudying *is a personal and lonely task. And it demands active, concentrated participation. Your ability to concentrate is increased not only by your own attitude toward studying but by the physical conditions around you. Most people can study almost anywhere—if the subject fascinates them. But they have difficulty concentrating on something they consider uninteresting—especially if there are many distractions around them. Where you study is important.*

You need to eliminate as many distractions as possible if you are to focus your attention on studying. You probably have assured your parents more than once that you can study effectively as you watch a rock video, eat meals and snacks, or talk on the phone to your friends. You have probably also told them that having your friends around you helps your concentration. But don't believe it. Studies have shown that all of these things detract from careful concentration. You can in fact study with such distractions. But your study will be both less efficient and less effective.

## The Best Conditions

The requirements for study surroundings will be different for each student. What you need to do is to discover the kind of environment that will give you the best atmosphere for study. Just having the ideal physical conditions will enable you to concentrate for longer periods of time. It is important to have a place that you find comfortable, whether it is a lounge chair with a TV tray beside it or a straight back chair and desk. Make sure that your physical surroundings are free from distracting influences. However, you will need to do more in order to create your best study conditions.

Everything that most people take for granted must be considered. The air circulation must be good. Improper circulation of air in a study area will cause lack of oxygen. Lack of sufficient oxygen will reduce both your mental and physical alertness. And there is no question that you must be both mentally and physically alert for maximum learning to take place. Insufficient light and glare from desk tops and papers can produce eye fatigue. Eye fatigue also reduces learning efficiency. Noise also has a distracting influence on your studying. Just hearing the background noise of a television or a radio can reduce your concentration. How you feel will also affect how well you can study. You cannot study well if you are tired or hungry, if your eyes burn, or if you are nauseated. Under any of these conditions, you need to break and eliminate the distraction before returning to your studying.

## Find Your Place

Keep in mind that your study area is yours and yours alone. Choose it wisely. You should set aside a particular place as your area. And you should always use that place for serious study sessions. The place could be a corner of your bedroom, a den, or if space permits, a separate room that is intended only for work, study, and concentration. This is not the place to have a television set, your stereo outfit, or things relating to your hobby. It must not become a recreational area.

*You should set aside a particular place as your study area. And you should always use that place for serious study sessions.*

You should feel that while you are in this area you will not be distracted until you have completed your studies as scheduled. You must build a mind-set for study in this particular room: no visitors, no phone calls, and no other distractions until you have finished your study task.

In addition, be sure that the place you choose is away from normal traffic patterns. For example, it would be a mistake to locate your study area in a place other members of your family would have to cross to get to the bathroom. It would also be a good idea to choose a room with a door that could be closed if necessary. You must adapt your study area to your particular needs.

## Adequate Lighting

Check the lighting in the place you have selected as your special study area. Take into account the direction from which the light comes. It is best to have the main light source come from the side to avoid glare. Make all the necessary adjustments so that you will have adequate, uniform lighting over your textbook pages or on the area you will be using for writing. Good lighting decreases the tension developed during reading. But be careful not to have excessively bright lights. Lights that are too bright can reduce reading speed and cause eye strain. The best kind of lighting is indirect or diffused lighting.

*The best kind of lighting is indirect or diffused lighting.*

## Appropriate Temperature

Room temperature also affects learning. If your area is too hot, it could make you sleepy. On the other hand, if the area is too cold, your discomfort will lessen your ability to concentrate on your studying. For most students, the proper temperature for a study area should not exceed about 70° F. (21° C). This temperature is ideal for peak mental and physical alertness. A relative humidity of about 50 per cent is also desirable.

## Suitable Noise Level

For most students, almost any form of noise is distracting. The noise level in your study area can affect your performance. Studying with either your radio on or the television set turned up will certainly not help you make the best use of your study time. However, playing soft music in your study area might help you drown out other interfering noises that disrupt your thought processes.

## Sufficient Comfort

Another thing that affects your learning is your posture. Traditionally, it was thought that the only way to study was to sit up straight at a desk. Now it is believed that some students may need a more informal position on a chair, bed, or on the floor. Many classrooms are no longer insisting that students spend all their time sitting at their desks. One caution—you can choose a position that is so comfortable that you soon fall asleep. Be careful that you do not become too comfortable when you study.

## Discover What You Need

Students study best under many different conditions. You need to discover exactly what kind of environment you need for your studying. Carefully read the statements under each heading and choose the one that best describes the conditions that will help you study effectively.

### Light Level

1.  I need strong bright light on my work.
2.  I need light on my work, but it doesn't have to be bright.
3.  I need the lights to be very low.
4.  I need daylight rather than artificial light.

### Temperature Level

1.  I need a very warm, almost hot, study area.
2.  I need a warm area that does not require my wearing a sweater.
3.  I need a cool area.
4.  I need a very cool area.

### Noise Level

1.  I need to hear the loud sounds of records, radio, or television.
2.  I need to hear soft background noise.
3.  I need a relatively quiet study environment.
4.  I need absolute quiet.

### Comfort Level

1. I need to sit on a hard chair at a desk.
2. I need to sit on a comfortable chair at a desk.
3. I need to sit on a comfortable chair, couch, or bed.
4. I need to lie on a bed, a couch, or the floor.

Now that you know the environmental conditions that you need for studying, you are ready to set up a study area in your home. It should also be pointed out that to maintain concentration while you are studying, you must also pay attention to your own physical condition. You need to eat three regular, well-balanced meals a day, exercise frequently, and get proper amounts of sleep.

## Your Study Area

*Once you have found your study area, you need to arrange it so that it is ready for you to use at any time.*

You don't need to prepare a soundproof cell in your home with plain white walls for your study area. Still, you do need to arrange a definite area where you will study each time. Otherwise, you will waste your study time trying to become familiar with the sights and sounds of a new area every time you study.

Many students have a problem trying to find a study area. If you share a room with a brother or a sister, both of you could agree to study at the same time in opposite corners. Or you could get up early in the morning and study when your brother or sister is asleep. When you are looking for a study area, don't overlook the kitchen, dining room, or living room. If your home is too crowded or noisy, you could go to the library or ask permission to study at the home of a friend or relative who has more space.

## Setting up Your Work Area

Once you have found your study area, you need to arrange it so that it is ready for you to use at any time. Begin by selecting and arranging the furniture. It is important that you have a permanent work surface. Ask yourself these questions when you are selecting your work surface:

1.  Does the work surface allow for good posture?

    The work surface should be at a height that will permit you to study in a comfortable upright posture with your feet touching the floor. The chair should provide support for your lower back and shoulders. Improper support will lead to tension and fatigue. And tension and fatigue will distract you.

2.  Does it have adequate top surface?

    Your work surface should be large enough to allow you to spread out your notebook, books, and other needed materials like a typewriter, a computer, or a calculator.

3.  Is there sufficient storage space?

    All the materials that you need should be within easy reach. You will not be able to concentrate if you must constantly leave your work area to get study materials.

4.  Is it placed to reduce distractions?

    Your work surface should be placed against a wall. There is much less chance for distraction if you face a wall while studying. It is also helpful if there is a window nearby for sunlight and fresh air.

## Organizing Your Study Area

Once you have selected the best work surface, take extra time to make sure that the lighting and temperature fit your needs. Then, before your first study session, remove all objects that might steal your attention, including papers and books not related to your study needs. The fewer items you have available to tempt you, the better the opportunity for concentration. Each time you finish studying, straighten up the work area so it is always ready to be used immediately.

## Getting Your Supplies

No study area is complete if it is not equipped with all the things needed to get the job done. You never see a carpenter's workbench without basic tools like a hammer, saw, and nails. A dictionary is just as important to a student as a hammer is to a carpenter. You cannot turn in class assignments that contain misspelled words. A thesaurus is also a good reference book to have available.

There are certain study aids that you need to use all the time and there are others that you may use only occasionally. Look at the list below and determine the things that you will need for your study area:

| **Basic Supplies** | **Less Needed Supplies** |
|---|---|
| _____ paper | _____ paints |
| _____ pencils | _____ stencils |
| _____ erasers | _____ stapler |
| _____ pens | _____ colored paper |
| _____ dictionary | _____ atlas |
| _____ ruler | _____ compass |
| _____ paper clips | _____ protractor |
| _____ rubber bands | _____ envelopes |
| _____ scissors | _____ colored pencils |
| _____ Scotch tape | _____ gum eraser |
| _____ scrap paper | _____ typewriter |
| _____ folders | _____ typing paper |
| _____ thesaurus | _____ graph paper |
| _____ calculator | _____ encyclopedias |
| _____ glue | _____ computer |
| _____ pencil sharpener | _____ crayons |

If the basic supplies are not within your reach when you want them, you will break your concentration by having to leave your work area to search for them. You may also be sidetracked and not get back to work until much later.

## Coping with Distractions

You must try to eliminate distractions that are caused by your family or friends. Unless you tell these people that what they are doing is bothering you, these distractions may never disappear. Point out nicely to your brother that his gum popping near your study area drives you nuts. Explain to your dad that when he turns up the television in the next room, you lose your concentration. And as much as you enjoy talking to your grandfather, explain to him that when you are in your study area, you prefer not to interrupt your studying for a chat.

If there are other students in your family having the same problems, perhaps you can create a quiet time at your house so that everyone can study without so many distractions. Keep in mind that you are not living in an isolation booth and that some reasonable family noise is to be expected and must be tolerated.

*Perhaps you can create a quiet time at your house so that everyone can study without so many distractions.*

### Making a List of Distractions

When you start to use your study area, make a list of all the distractions that interfere with your studying. When you have finished studying, think of ways that you can prevent these distractions from happening again. Here is a list that one student made:

| Distractions | Ways to Eliminate |
|---|---|
| Skippy barked and needed to be taken out for a walk. | Walk the dog before beginning to study. |
| Starving—had to heat a pizza. | Prepare a snack before long study sessions. |
| Brother played loud rock music. | Try to negotiate with him. |

## Avoiding Distractions

There are other things besides the actions of your family that will cause you to become distracted from studying. Unplug the phone so you won't be tempted to call or talk to friends. Draw the curtains or pull down the shade if your work area overlooks a busy street or a play area. Otherwise, you may find yourself gazing out the window rather than concentrating on your studying. If someone is vacuuming the hall, watching television in the family room, or holding a club meeting in the basement, try to mask out these sounds by playing soft background music. If the noise level is always high in your home, consider wearing headphones while you are studying.

*If the noise level is always high in your home, consider wearing headphones while you are studying.*

## Studying at School

The place where you do most of your studying is not at home where you can arrange an area just the way you want it. You study mostly at school where you may not have much say about where you study. Your teachers probably give you some study time for every subject that you are taking, so your study time at school quickly adds up.

It isn't very difficult to think of all the things that can distract you from studying in the typical classroom. So much seems to be going on all the time that it is scarcely ever boring to look around the room. Also, many different noises can capture your attention as you try to study an assignment. Your ears may hear feet shuffling, papers turning, pencils scratching, books being dropped, desks opening and closing, students whispering, and many other things. It is not easy to ignore other noises that drift into the classroom from outside, such as locker doors slamming shut, gym classes playing games, and lawns being mowed. You must learn how to block out these distractions while studying at school.

# Reducing Distractions at School

The easiest way to reduce distractions that are interfering with your studying at school is to simply sit in the front row in every classroom. If this is not possible, try to sit as close to the front of the room as you can. When you sit in the middle or the back of a classroom, you are distracted by all the people in front of you. You can't help noticing what they are doing. Up front it's just you, the blackboard, and the teacher. Besides, there are added benefits to taking this usually unpopular seating that few students want. The teacher will believe that you are showing interest in the class and that you are eager to learn. In addition, teachers will often show more interest in students sitting up front and will help them more frequently on assignments. You will also find that you pay closer attention to what the teacher is saying, which in turn will make your studying easier.

*Sit in the front row in every classroom.*

# Handling Serious Problems

Earlier in this section, you found out what environmental conditions you needed in order to do your best serious studying. If you found that even the lowest noise level distracted you from studying, you might consider asking your teachers if you could work in a quiet corner of the classroom. Since many students are distracted by all the things that they see happening in the classroom, some schools now have study carrels available in the back of the room that can be used for individual study. Don't hesitate to use one if you need it.

If you have serious problems studying in the classroom, be sure to discuss them with your teachers. They should be able to make some adjustments in the classroom environment to make studying easier for you. Teachers are becoming increasingly aware that the same conditions for study are not ideal for all students. That is why you sometimes now see students lying on the floor, sitting in comfortable chairs, eating snacks, working in groups, and doing other things that were once considered inappropriate during study periods.

## Studying in Study Hall

As the name suggests, you are expected to study in a study hall. And it can be an excellent place to study for tests, prepare for class, or do your homework. Yet study halls are not the perfect place for everyone to study, because like classrooms, they can have loads of distractions that interfere with your efforts to study. For example, if the study hall is in a cafeteria, you may hear far more noise than you can block out as lunch is prepared or dishes are washed. You may also find that the temperature is too hot, the lighting is too dim, and the chairs are too small. Unfortunately, you may have to spend so much effort blocking out distractions that you feel utterly fatigued after an hour in a study hall.

When given a choice, always select a smaller study hall rather than a larger one, since you may be able to have some say in the way it is set up. As in the classroom, you should try to sit in the front row or toward the front of a study hall to minimize the number of distractions that you can see.

*When given a choice, always select a smaller study hall rather than a larger one.*

## Studying in a Library

If there are too many distractions in your home or school that simply cannot be eliminated so that you can study, go to the library. Libraries are intended to be quiet places. Phones don't ring, loud music doesn't blare, and most people try to be quiet. In fact, with only a few exceptions, libraries are good places for studying.

When you are studying in a library, try to find the spot that is closest to your ideal place to study. There are a lot of options in today's libraries. So look around for the quiet corner, the study carrel, the comfortable chair, or the large, flat surface for spreading out your books. If you are going to a library to use certain materials like reference books, magazines, newspapers, or microfilm, then choose a spot by these materials so your study time won't be spent wandering around the library. Another reason that the library is an excellent place to study is that librarians are usually very willing to help you find any information that you may need. Also, a wealth of material is almost at your fingertips.

When you go to the library or any place other than your usual study area, take a few minutes to accustom yourself to the unfamiliar environment. Look at the people and the furniture, settle down in your chair, and listen to the sounds until you feel at home. The next time you go to the library, sit in the same place so that you will not have to spend as much time settling down to study.

## Your Best Place to Study

Whether you are studying at home, at school, or in the library, you need to know exactly what kind of environment helps you to study most efficiently and effectively. For most students, the traditional guidelines of a quiet place free from distractions, a desk or table and a chair, light that falls evenly on what you are reading, and an appropriate temperature describe the most favorable surroundings. Certain study materials, like a dictionary and a thesaurus, should also be close at hand. And some provision should be made for keeping notes and work papers in an orderly arrangement so they can be found in a second. A bookshelf and drawers for storing materials is handy and encourages neatness and efficiency. Because acquiring knowledge is important to every person, it is wise to set up the study area that will best help you study.

*How to make a study schedule and adapt it to your everyday life is the subject of this section.*

play

5

APRI

11

19

18

7

25

24

30

TUESDAY

15

MARCH
S M T W T F S
            1
2 3 4 5 6 7 8
9 10 11 12 13 14 15
16 17 18 19 20 21 22
23 24 25 26 27 28 29
30 31

MAY
S M T W T F S
      1 2 3
4 5 6 7 8 9 10
11 12 13 14 15 16 17
18 19 20 21 22 23 24
25 26 27 28 29 30 31

TEST
10:00 AM
Room 101

# The Best Time to Study

You have a test on Friday covering World War I. Will you be able to go to bed early Thursday night, or will you be staying up late, frantically cramming dates and facts about battles into your head? On October 1, the science teacher assigns a report on molds that will be due on October 15. Will you hand the report in on October 14, October 15, or October 16? Every day you have homework in math. Will you usually finish it during class study time or study hall? Will you finish it with the rest of your homework? Or will you work on it during breakfast or just before class starts? Will you turn it in after class?

How did you answer these questions? Do your answers describe a student whose life is one long struggle to get schoolwork done on time? Are you a student who makes deadlines at times, but fails miserably at other times in spite of your best intentions? Are you a well-organized student who is on top of your work—a student who is following a study schedule? Research continues to show that successful students usually work according to some kind of formal plan.

## A Study Schedule

You can get by without a study schedule, but you won't be able to do much more than that. Regardless of how smart you are or how quickly you learn, you are not placing value on either your time or your education unless you have some kind of formal plan for organizing your study time. Haphazard study habits are inefficient, and inefficiency wastes valuable time. Without a plan of action or a study schedule, many assignments will be left incomplete or skipped over altogether.

There is probably not a student anywhere who has not said "I didn't have time" to finish the book report, memorize the poem, or do any of a million other things required for school. Do students offer this tired, old excuse because they really don't have time in spite of their best intentions? Rarely is the answer "yes." Most often, the answer is procrastination or putting off until tomorrow what you are too lazy to do today. Students put off schoolwork to do something else, and then it is too late to do more than a sloppy job of studying. Your education will suffer unless you bring order to your studying and get in the habit of completing tasks on time. Good work habits, which mean having a study schedule and following it, are one of the keys to success in school.

Good work habits will help you not only in school, but also after your school career is finished. People who are successful in any field almost always have good work habits. If you aim at success in school and in life, you will need to be self-directed and assume personal responsibility for the use of your time. A planned study schedule is the best way to make sure you are using your time most efficiently.

Many students do not believe that they will have more time for study and pleasure rather than less if they organize their time. They say, "Even if I plan, there still isn't enough time to complete what I have to do." This statement is nothing more than a crutch—an excuse to avoid making a commitment to education. Time schedules work. Every family operates on a time budget, whether a schedule is written down or not. Work time, mealtime, bedtime, recreation time, shopping time—all fall into regular daily or weekly time slots. So should studying, and when it does, time spent studying becomes time spent productively. The first step in developing a plan is to gather information about how you are spending your time.

## Where Do Your Hours Go?

Your school day is organized for you. Things seem to go fine from 8 A.M. to 3 P.M. There is a set time for English, math, science, social studies, lunch, gym, and so on. However, things change when you walk out the school door. All of a sudden, you are on your own—able to spend time as you choose. If you subtract time for sleeping, you probably have about sixty hours per week that is your own free time.

How do you use your free time? Have you ever analyzed what you do with all that time? Do you spend a lot of time watching television, listening to music, or just fooling around? Do you spend too much time on a particular extracurricular activity, such as sports? For most students, it really is a mystery how time gets away. It takes courage and action to analyze how you use and abuse your free time. You must have the courage to admit to yourself when you are wasting time.

*You must have the courage to admit to yourself when you are wasting time.*

## Solving the Mystery

The first step toward solving the mystery of where your time goes is to find out exactly what you are doing with your time. Keep a list for one week of everything you do. This list should include class attendance, studying, going to a movie, or talking on the phone—everything you do for a week. Until you know how you are spending your time, you will be unable to judge whether or not you are using your free time wisely.

Think carefully before you write anything down on your list. You are in the process of gathering valuable information. This information will be used to develop a plan for more efficient use of time. Make the list as detailed as possible. And be honest with yourself.

Begin with the time you wake up in the morning. Continue by filling in the hours until bedtime. A list of time spent during a typical school day might look something like this:

### Use-of-Time Chart
### Monday, October 9

| Hours | Activities |
|---|---|
| 7:00–7:30 | Dress and eat breakfast |
| 7:30–8:00 | Walk to school |

| Hours | Activities |
| --- | --- |
| 8:00–9:00 | English class—fell asleep |
| 9:00–10:00 | Social studies class—did math homework |
| 10:00–11:00 | Study hall—went to the library—talked to friends |
| 11:00–11:30 | Skipped lunch to do math homework |
| 11:30–12:30 | Math class—had a test |
| 12:30–1:30 | Biology—did a lab |
| 1:30–2:30 | Art—worked on still life |
| 2:30–3:30 | Gym class |
| 3:30–4:00 | Had a snack (15 minutes) and got ready for tennis practice (15 minutes) |
| 4:00–6:00 | Tennis practice |
| 6:00–6:15 | Rode home |
| 6:15–6:30 | Relaxed |
| 6:30–7:00 | Dinner—did dishes |
| 7:00–8:00 | Rode bicycle with friends |
| 8:00–8:30 | Talked on the phone |
| 8:30–9:00 | Exercised |
| 9:00–10:00 | Watched TV |
| 10:00–10:30 | Fixed snack—started homework |
| 10:30–11:00 | Did homework |
| 11:00–11:30 | Watched TV in bed |

After you have kept a list of your activities for a day, you need to divide the hours into the following categories. The sample list would be subdivided in this way:

**Total Time Available—16½ hours**

<u> 6 </u>  Time in class

<u> 1 </u>  Time studying outside of class

<u> 4 </u>  Time for organized activities (transportation, meals, sports, and so on)

<u>2½</u>  Time for social activities

<u> 3 </u>  Time not accounted for by the above activities

When you have made a list for each day of a week, you should compile and record weekly totals for the categories.

## Analyzing Your Time Chart

The time chart above looks very full; however, the student has three hours that cannot be accounted for besides the two and one-half hours that were spent for social activities. As you inspect the chart, it becomes obvious that this student is having problems settling down to study. Notice how the student spent so much time visiting instead of studying. Also notice how the student wasted time in English class by sleeping and in the social studies class by trying to do work for another class. The student's time after school was too full to study. But in the evening, the student put off studying until it was really too late to begin. With better planning, this student could have had more time to lift weights, watch TV, and even get to bed earlier.

## How You Spend Your Time

Time is precious. Its use should be planned to gain the greatest advantage. Time can be used to aid and benefit worthwhile activities. Or time can be frittered away with nothing gained. When you are finally able to examine your time charts for a whole week, you should be able to recognize at a glance where your time has been going. You may be surprised at the amount of time that you have wasted or are unable to account for. Don't get discouraged. Yours is not an uncommon problem. But it takes desire and will to solve this problem. For you must really want to use your time more productively and must have the determination to stick to whatever time schedule you prepare for yourself.

## Early Bird or Night Owl?

Now that you know how you have been spending your time, there is one more thing that you need to do before beginning to set up your own study schedule. Decide what time of day you function most efficiently. Some people bound out of bed—ready for anything. Others come alive at midmorning, after lunch, or late afternoon. A few people don't begin to really wake up until after dark. And of course, there are those who can function equally well any time of day. Many students have periods of peak efficiency when they feel alert, think clearly, and perform at their very best. If you have such a time, you should try to schedule as much of your studying during this time as possible.

## Planning Your Time Chart

First of all, be cautious about getting overly enthusiastic or making commitments that cannot be met. A building goes up a brick or a board at a time. Don't convince yourself that all you need to do is to go to bed later or get up earlier, using the extra time for studying, and all will be well. Time for adequate rest is as important to a study schedule as any other item. Don't promise yourself that from now on you will study during the time between the end of school and bedtime each day, with perhaps an hour off for dinner. You know that this is unlikely and that one needs more than just meal breaks from routine each day. Be sensible and realistic in planning your study schedule. You cannot copy another person's schedule, because each

*You must develop a working study schedule that will meet your study needs.*

schedule must be a personal one. Your schedule must meet your own needs.

Begin planning your study schedule by looking over the use-of-time chart that you prepared. The information shown on this chart will tell you what your present schedule is. Ask yourself the following questions while reviewing the chart:

- Do I plan in advance how I will spend my daily study time?

- Do I schedule study periods so that they precede and/ or follow a subject being studied?

- Do I study consistently during free hours of the day to avoid last-minute cramming?

- Do I provide for additional time in my daily, weekly, and semester schedules for term papers and other special projects?

- Do I provide time for review of lessons on a daily and a weekly basis?

- Do I schedule my social activities so that they do not interfere with study time?

- Do I schedule daily periods for recreation?

It is very likely that your answer to most of these questions will be "no." And this should convince you that you must develop a working study schedule that will meet your study needs.

## The General Principles of Planning

No matter what grade you are in, there are certain general principles that you will want to follow in setting up your study schedule. The first principle is to set your goals. Know exactly what you are trying to accomplish. For most students, the major goal of a study schedule is to handle daily assignments in an organized way. While preparing your schedule, keep these other principles in mind:

- Plan for required periods of time. Classes at school, mealtimes, and required activities such as music lessons, regular doctor's appointments, and so forth should be blocked in first so that you have a good idea of what time is available for other activities.

- Plan for emergencies. Be ready to make adjustments in your schedule for emergencies. Include an occasional free period in your schedule. This free period could be used to make up scheduled study periods lost because of some emergency.

- Plan ample time for study. Some subjects will need little or no study time. But others may require more than the usual amount of time. You must be the judge of how much time certain subjects need. After a period of intensive study, do not schedule another intensive study period immediately afterward. Include a rest period. Without scheduled rest periods, learning suffers. Try to study within the time limits you have set for yourself. The kind of studying you do is more important than the amount of studying you do. And above all, get started. Don't waste time during your study period.

- Plan a study session after a particular class. Planning the study of a subject immediately after the class period enables you to work on the assignment while it is fresh in your mind. Whenever this is not possible, then plan to schedule a study session as soon after the class period as possible.

- Plan for your learning style. Each student has his or her own learning style. Are you an early bird who seems to learn best in the morning, or are you a night owl who seems to learn best in the after-dinner hours? If you are an early bird, then plan to include much of your intensive study or review during morning hours. You may like to schedule your time so that you study before breakfast.

- Plan to study difficult subjects when you are most alert. Make an extra effort to eliminate distractions when you are studying these subjects. Some students like to study difficult subjects before easier subjects and others prefer to begin with easier subjects and warm up to the more difficult ones. There is no particular advantage to either approach.

*Plan to study the same subjects at the same times each day.*

- Plan to study the same subjects at the same times each day. Consistency is important. If you know that at 10 A.M. each day from Monday to Friday you will be studying science, then you will find that you are prepared mentally to study science at that time. You need mental preparation to concentrate.

- Plan for review sessions. Set aside some time for review of each subject. Also, plan for additional review time before a quiz or a test.

- Plan for some free time in your schedule. Every scheduled hour of the day need not be set aside for studying. Some free time in your schedule will permit you to take care of emergencies, schedule more time for activities of your liking, or have additional time for extra study of a particular subject.

- Plan for leisure, recreation, and chores. "All work and no play makes Jack a dull boy," as the old saying goes. Physical activity is just as important as mental activity. It is important that you set aside some time for physical activity in your schedule. This time need not be for an active sport. Taking a brisk walk can be a satisfying break between study sessions.

- Plan for specific tasks. After you have blocked in your specific subjects and other activities, be sure to provide space to write descriptions of specific tasks. These descriptions should include such things as pages to read, number of problems to complete, and so on. Your entries should look something like the following:

Math: Read pp. 17–18.
    Do problems 1–12.
    Review for quiz.

English: Write a paragraph describing
    something beautiful

- Plan to review your study schedule frequently. Do not throw out your study schedule because it is not meeting your needs. Instead, revise it frequently until it becomes a plan that you can easily follow.

## Allotting Time for Study

Most educators feel that the way in which time after school is spent is vital to the success or failure of many students. These hours are rarely bare of scheduled activities. You might have athletic practice, rehearsals for school plays, music lessons, chores to do at home, or a job. Even so, some of the time after school should be allotted to study, if possible.

The first hour or so after school might be left free as a time to break away from routine. During that time, you might play ball, talk with friends, work at a hobby, come home and watch television, or engage in some other relaxing activity.

This still leaves some time before dinner for other things. And you might slot some of this time for studying. This, in fact, might be an appropriate time slot for free study; a few moments you can use if and when extra study is needed.

### Evening Television

In slotting your time, it would be unrealistic to rule out all evening television until 9 P.M. or so. But special programs that you must see don't appear for hours on end every night of the week. So, if you find you need additional time for study in the evening, control 'the amount of time you devote to television. Make choices and set priorities. After all, learning to make choices and to set priorities is an important part of growing up. And so is learning to live with your choices and sticking to your priorities.

### Studying in and out of School

How much time you should allot to studying in and out of school depends on how you are doing and, to some extent, on current academic demands. An upcoming quiz or test might demand additional study time for a week before. Ordinarily, though, it is wise to allot a particular amount of time, both in school and at home, to a particular school subject.

As for total study time, one rule of thumb is to plan for at least three to five hours of study per week for each subject. This can include study time given in class. Keep in mind that such time requirements vary from student to student and from subject to subject. Some experimentation will have to be done before you discover how much time you should allot to a given subject.

*Plan for at least three to five hours of study per week for each subject.*

### Scheduling Problems

A part-time job naturally takes away from the time available for other things, including study. When making a study schedule, a part-time job forces an even closer examination of priorities and goals.

This can be a difficult problem. Work experience is valuable to a person in junior or senior high school. It serves as an introduction to the working world. Work experience can help build a person's sense of responsibility. Investigations have suggested that many students with part-time jobs and a sensible study schedule make better use of their time than those with neither. Students who have many things to do tend to be much more serious about planning how to spend their time.

On the other hand, a job can serve as an excuse for not studying. Whether used as an excuse or not, it can still be a cause of poor performance in school. Also, even though a person may keep up well with both work and school, these responsibilities often cut severely into the time available for recreation and rest.

Here, as in many other situations, your ability to manage both schoolwork and a part-time job depends on you. This is a situation you must monitor carefully. It is also a situation that will benefit especially from the use of a well-planned study schedule.

### Studying on Weekends

Studying is also an individual problem requiring individualized solutions. Some students budget and make such efficient use of their time during the school week that weekends remain entirely free for recreation and relaxation. Other students cannot do so well.

Most students reserve Friday night and Saturday for social events, miscellaneous chores, and shopping. Many students use large portions of their weekends for watching televised athletic events. Students often schedule weekend study on Sunday afternoon or Sunday evening, when thoughts usually turn to another week of school. For a good many students, this is sufficient. But, again, much depends on the individual. In making up a weekly schedule, though, you should decide about how to study on weekends and stay with the schedule you make.

## Making Your Study Schedule

Keeping in mind all the previously mentioned guidelines and suggestions for allotting your time, you are now ready to make your own personalized study schedule. Incidentally, it is important that you be realistic when preparing your schedule. A common mistake made by many students preparing their first study schedule is to try to do the impossible. These students set aside every free hour for study and provide little or no time for rest and relaxation.

Such a schedule quickly becomes a grind. If you make this mistake, you will probably not stick to your schedule long enough to find the value in it. Keep in mind that your schedule is intended to make your work easier and to give you greater satisfaction and freedom than you now have.

Earlier in this section, you looked at a chart that showed how a student had spent a day. The student was having all kinds of problems settling down to study. What follows is the study schedule that this same student made. Study this sample for some guidelines as to what your study schedule should be like. Note how this student now has sufficient time for both studying and socializing. And the student has not made an unrealistic schedule that cannot possibly be followed.

## Study Schedule for One Week

| Hours | Mon. | Tues. | Wed. | Thurs. | Fri. | Sat. | Sun. |
|---|---|---|---|---|---|---|---|
| 7:00 | dress and eat breakfast | | | | | dress | church, personal activity, watch TV, free time, and special study |
| 7:30 | walk to school | | | | | breakfast | |
| 8:00 | English | English | English | English | English | tennis practice | |
| 9:00 | soc. st. | soc. st. | soc. st. | soc. st. | soc. st. | | |
| 10:00 | study hall—study social studies and do math homework | | | | | free time | |
| 11:00 | lunch | lunch | lunch | lunch | lunch | | |
| 11:30 | math | math | math | math | math | lunch | |
| 12:30 | biology | biology | biology | biology | biology | job | |
| 1:30 | art | art | art | art | art | | |
| 2:30 | P.E. | P.E. | P.E. | P.E. | P.E. | | |
| 3:30 | snack and get ready for tennis practice | | | | | | |
| 4:00 5:00 | tennis practice | | | | | free time | |
| 6:00 | return home—relax | | | | | | |
| 6:30 | dinner—help with dishes | | | | | | |
| 7:00 | study English | study English | study English | study English | social activities | | study English |
| 7:30 | study biology | study biology | study biology | study biology | | | study biology |
| 8:00 | lift weights | | | | | | free time |
| 8:30 | special study period for review or test | | | | | | |
| 9:00 | free time: watch TV, talk on phone, special study, and so forth | | | | | | |

## Getting Organized

By now, you should be convinced of the advantages of scheduling your time, and you should be eager to start making your own study schedule. It is easiest to make a schedule if you have a ready-made book that already has each day divided into hours. A particularly good choice for a schedule book is a teacher's plan book which is already subdivided for the school year.

Begin your new daily schedule with the time you get up. First enter the items already budgeted for a typical week—classes, lunch periods, and so on. Don't forget to pencil in regular after-school and evening activities and all the other things that are going to happen that week, such as doctor's appointments, athletic contests, and music lessons. Then look at the empty slots. These are the primary time slots a student might use for studying.

Next, decide which subjects should be studied regularly in each time slot. For example, if there is a free period just before English class, allot that free period to preparing the English assignment for that day. A particular assignment might require more than one class period's preparation. But at least you have one block of time available for preparation.

## The Long-Range Schedule

Besides a daily time schedule, you should prepare a long-range schedule or calendar that lets you write down dates for such things as ball games, semester tests, vacations, dances, term paper deadlines, and other important events. If you are using a yearlong plan book, you can just write these items on your regular time schedule in red ink. What follows is an example of such a long-range schedule. It was written by the same student who made the earlier charts. Unpleasant surprises will not ruin this student's study schedule, as dates for future tests and assignments are noted.

## Calendar of Important Days

| WEEK | 1st | 2nd | 3rd | 4th | 5th | 6th |
|---|---|---|---|---|---|---|
| **DATES** | 10/16 to 10/22 | 10/23 to 10/29 | 10/30 to 11/5 | 11/6 to 11/12 | 11/13 to 11/19 | 11/20 to 11/26 |
| **English** | quiz 10/20 | | report 11/5 | | speech 11/15 | |
| **social studies** | | | test 10/30 | | | test 11/20 |
| **math** | quiz 10/21 | quiz 10/28 | test 11/4 | quiz 11/11 | quiz 11/18 | quiz 11/25 |
| **biology** | | lab report 10/24 | test 11/4 | | lab report 11/14 | |
| **art** | | | still life 11/5 | | | |
| **P.E.** | | | test 10/30 | | | |
| **swim meets** | home 10/21 | away 10/28 | away 11/4 | regionals 11/11 | sectionals 11/18 | finals 11/25 |
| **social** | play 10/22 | bsktbl game 10/29 | | bsktbl game 11/12 | | |
| **doctor** | | | | | dentist 11/14 | |
| **clubs** | | letter 10/24 | | | | letter 11/21 |

## Flexibility

No schedule is immune from adjustment. Events get postponed, something unexpected comes up, finishing an assignment proves more difficult than anticipated, and the schedule has to change. Keep these possibilities in mind, and always remember the need for flexibility.

Flexibility is a key element in planning. Budgeting time is not intended to encase you in a straitjacket. Rather, the goal of planning your time is to help you take into consideration the various demands that school and other activities make and to balance these demands against your own needs. A realistic schedule provides adequate time for productive study, and it also allows ample time for relaxation, recreation, the pursuit of hobbies, and for just fooling around.

Help yourself stick to your new schedule by building a system of rewards into it. Also, tell everyone your plans so that you will feel additional pressure to follow the schedule. Once you have followed a schedule for a couple of weeks, you may never do without one again, because you will find that you have fewer worries, more time for fun and friends, and better grades.

# IV STUDY AIDS

*There are many items around your home, in your classroom, and at the local library that can help when you study. Such study aids are described in this section.*

SHAPES OF SOME TYPES OF CELLS

Muscle Cells

Blood Cell

Skin Cells

**CELL**

This article describes the cell and how it works. For further information, see also the WORLD BOOK articles on HEREDITY and LIFE.

**Looking at a Cell**

More than 1½ million species of plants and animals live on the earth. They differ greatly in shape, in size, and in the way they live. But they all have one thing in common—they are all made up of cells.

One of the most important tools scientists use to study cells is the microscope. An *optical microscope* can magnify a cell up to 2,000 times. An *electron microscope* can magnify a cell more than 200,000 times on photographic film. An ant magnified 200,000 times would be more than ½ mile (0.8 kilometer) long. But even with such tremendous magnification, the detailed structure of some cell parts still cannot be seen. See MICROSCOPE.

Another tool used to study cells is the *centrifuge*. This instrument separates the various substances in a mixture by whirling the chemical content and chemical reactions of study cells. Scientists first grind up the cells. Then they put the bits and pieces into a centrifuge and whirl them rapidly. The particles separate into layers. The heaviest particles settle at the bottom, and the lightest ones gather at the top. After they have been separated, the particles can be checked for their chemical content. See

... also use dyes to study cells. When various ... stained with certain dyes, these parts ... a microscope.

... may be shaped like cubes, saucers ... orkscrews, rods, ... *unicellular* (one-cell ... cells. They ...

## THE STRUCTURES OF A CELL

Cells differ in size, shape, and function. There is no "typical" cell. Yet almost all cells have many things in common. For this reason, it is helpful to imagine "typical" plant and animal cells like these.

Lysosome

Centrioles

Mitochondrion

Golgi Bodies

Vacuole

Cell Membrane

**Nucleus**
Nucleolus
Nuclear Membrane
Chromosomes

Endoplasmic Reticulum
Ribosomes

Cell Wall

Chloroplast

"Typical" Animal Cell

Nerve Cell

Paramecium

*Shapes of cells*

*cubes, coils, boxes, snowflakes, corkscrews, rods, saucers, rectangles or blobs of jelly.*

...tal number of cells it has, not on the size of...
...n elephant is a giant compared with a mouse...
it has trillions more cells, not because its cells a...

### Inside A Living Cell

We have seen that cells differ greatly in size, in shap... and in the special jobs they do. But we can imagine... typical living cell that has the features found in alm... all cells except those of bacteria and blue-green alg...

Such a cell can be thought of as a tiny chemical f... It has a control center that tells it what to do a... has power plants for generating energy; and... ...ry for making its products or performing...

...called the *cell membrane* or *plas*... ...ell and separates it from its su... ...main parts: (1) the nucleu... ...that directs the...

...life activities take place there. Many tiny structur... called *organelles* are located in the cytoplasm. Each... ...particular job to do. These organelles are called... ...a, *lysosomes*, the *endoplasmic reticulum*... ...bodies. ...are the power producers of... ...hundreds of mitochondri... ...to produce almost... ...do its work... ...boti...

...lysosomes help...
...acteria.
...n is a com...
...in the c...
...nes ar...
...tiny...
R...

# Study Aids

By now, you have established a study area in your home, and you have drawn up a study schedule. You are ready to sit down and get to work. Fortunately, a large number of study aids are available that you can use to make your task easier. You have probably included basic aids like the dictionary in your study area. But there are many other things around your home that will also help you with your studying. In fact, most homes have far more study aids than students realize. There are books, magazines, newspapers, television shows, and maps, to name just a few things found in almost every home that can be used while studying.

If you don't have sufficient study aids at home to complete your homework, the library is the place to go. Even the smallest library has encyclopedias, atlases, almanacs, catalogs, directories, and many different newspapers and magazines. In addition, most libraries can now obtain books and other materials from libraries all over the country through the interlibrary loan system.

## The Textbook

The study aid that will help you the most is your textbook. It is the one book that contains most of the information that teachers expect their students to learn about a subject. It is also usually organized in such a way that what you need to learn clearly stands out. First of all, the main ideas are almost always placed at the beginning of each chapter or section. Major points usually appear in the form of headings, and minor points are sometimes indicated. Often these headings are numbered for you. Each paragraph of many textbooks has topic and summary sentences. The topic sentence at the beginning of a paragraph gives the central idea of the paragraph. A summary sentence at the end of the paragraph wraps up the important idea. Each paragraph of this sort is already summarized for you. Textbooks usually also include some or all of the following aids to learning:

***Pictures, Charts, Diagrams, and Maps.*** These are included to give clearer meaning to materials in the chapter. The authors use them to visually reinforce important ideas.

***Important Ideas or Words.*** Ideas and definitions are sometimes printed in *italics* or in **boldface** type. This is done to draw your attention to these items because they are important ones to remember.

***Important Subpoints in Outline Form.*** Authors will often list important points in outline form for your convenience.

***Use of Explanatory Footnotes.*** Sometimes, authors will use footnotes to give added explanation of materials included in a chapter or section. Footnotes should be read carefully; they should not be ignored.

***Glossary.*** Many of the technical words that can cause confusion in a book are found in the glossary, which is really a miniature dictionary. The glossary usually tells you how a word is pronounced, the word's meaning, and the page number where the word first appears or is defined. What is especially helpful about the glossary is that it gives you the meanings of words as they are used in the textbook. For example, the word *product* in the glossary of a social studies textbook would be defined as something that is produced as a result of some work, while the same word in a math textbook would be defined as the result obtained by multiplying two or more numbers together.

***Index.*** The index lists in alphabetical order the topics covered in a textbook. For each topic, the page numbers where you can find information are given. If you want to know where in your grammar book to find information on adverbs, you should turn to the index. You will probably discover that adverbs are discussed on several pages of the textbook—perhaps in different chapters.

*The study aid that will help you most is your textbook.*

Study Aids

**The Table of Contents.** Like the index, the table of contents tells you about the topics in a book. The table of contents is far more general than an index, though. It just gives the basics on what information is in each chapter.

**The Bibliography.** At the end of a chapter or in the back of a textbook, you will often find lists of books or articles that you can read to find out more about certain topics. This listing is known as a bibliography, and it is usually prepared by the author. Textbook bibliographies are an excellent starting point for your research when you have to make reports or write papers.

*Textbooks are usually organized in such a way that what you need to learn clearly stands out.*

60

***End-of-Chapter Information and Exercises.*** Never ignore reading the materials at the end of a chapter. End-of-chapter information and exercises always make a good study guide for the chapter. There are usually lists of words that you should know, questions that you should be able to answer, and often even a summary of the main points of the chapter.

Not only are your textbooks the instructional tools you use the most, they also are your best study aid. Authors and publishers of textbooks have tried to make it easy for you to learn the material in their textbooks. Take advantage of all the help they give you.

# The Dictionary

You don't know how to spell *committee*. You wonder what a kiwi is. You don't have the vaguest idea how to pronounce the word *chasm*. These are the common, everyday reasons for consulting the dictionary. But a dictionary is more than a book in which you may find a word's spelling, meaning, and pronunciation. It is a storehouse of quick, easy-to-find information on other aspects of words.

For example, where did the gardenia get its name? The dictionary tells you that the gardenia is named after the Scottish naturalist Alexander Garden. It also tells you that a volt, a measure of electrical energy, is named after the Italian physicist Alessandro Volta. And the dictionary also tells you that a watt, a unit of electric power, gets its name from the Scottish engineer James Watt.

Besides telling you where a word comes from, the dictionary also informs you of the original meaning of parts of a word. The original meaning of the parts in the word *helicopter* are *heli* (spiral) + *pter* (wing). The word *helicopter* is closely tied to its parts, since it is kept aloft by *spiraling wings*. In the same way, the word *insect* comes from *in* (into) + *sect* (cut). If you look closely at an insect, such as an ant, you will see that it appears to be *cut into* sections or parts.

## Definitions Increase Your Vocabulary

*Your number-one use of the dictionary is to find out what words mean.*

Your number-one use of the dictionary is to find out what words mean. Many words have more than one meaning. Such words can be used in many different senses. The dictionary can help you not only to learn the meaning of new words but also to learn additional meanings for words you already know. Here are just a few ways the dictionary says you can use the word *about*. It may mean "dealing with" (*about* money), "nearly" (*about* empty), or "nearby" (somewhere *about* the garden). A recently ill person can now be up and *about*. Your friend may be *about* to leave. And a soldier may do an *about* face.

## Grammar Facts

The dictionary can give you considerable help with English grammar. It shows you how a word changes its meaning when a prefix or suffix is added to the root. *Meter* can change to *kilometer, diameter,* and *centimeter. Diction* can change to *dictionary.* And the dictionary gives you lists of words that begin with the same prefix, such as words beginning with *pre: precede, preface, preamble, prejudge, prehistoric, preoccupy,* and *prepay.*

The dictionary tells you whether a word is a noun, adjective, verb, or some other part of speech. In addition, the dictionary shows you how the word may be used in a phrase or sentence. The dictionary even tells you the plural form of nouns and the past tense of verbs. So when you don't know the plural of tricky words like *tomato, deer, buffalo,* or *ox,* look them up in the dictionary. Also consult the dictionary if you are not sure whether or not the past tense of *swim* is *swam* or *swum.*

## Using the English Language

The dictionary lists the synonyms and may list the antonyms for many words. Using the dictionary as a source for synonyms is especially important. If you look up a word in the dictionary and do not understand the definition, you can look at the synonyms for the word and perhaps find one you know well. This will give you a clue to the meaning of the word you looked up.

The dictionary can help you choose the right word for the right occasion. For example, the dictionary can help you decide whether to use the spelling *all right* or *alright.* It tells you that *all right* is the preferred spelling in formal usage and that *alright* is not generally acceptable. Of course, a word may be acceptable in one situation and not in another. For example, the word *ain't* is not acceptable in formal usage. But you sometimes hear the word *ain't* used in informal conversations. The dictionary lists the word as substandard, which means that it does not conform to the accepted forms of speech or writing.

The dictionary explains the use of words used in everyday, informal speech. It also includes slang and flashy or popular words that are used in a special way. These words are included because the dictionary is also a resource for understanding how language is being currently used.

## A Dictionary Entry

Look at all the helpful information a dictionary gives you, as shown below:

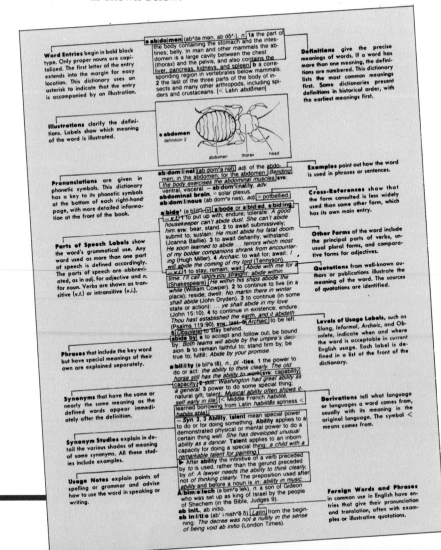

## Which Dictionary for You?

General dictionaries range in size from small pocket dictionaries to large multivolume or tabletop dictionaries. Each dictionary is designed to help certain types of readers. A sixth-grade student, for example, would not want all the information given in a dictionary that a college professor would use. So choose the dictionary that is appropriate for your grade level and your specific needs. Ask your teacher or your parents to help you select one.

*A thesaurus is a book of synonyms and antonyms.*

## The Thesaurus

It is not a good practice to use the same words repeatedly when you are writing. Have you ever been guilty of writing a passage like this?

> The big storm knocked over the big tree, which left a big hole in the ground.

If you are in the habit of overusing words, then the thesaurus is the book that you need to enliven your writing. Although the thesaurus looks like a dictionary, it is different. It is a book of synonyms and antonyms. A student using a thesaurus might have written the above sentence in a more imaginative fashion, like this:

> The huge storm knocked over the gigantic tree, which left an enormous hole in the ground.

A thesaurus will give you many substitutes for tired words like *big:*

> The plains are vast.
> Jimmy Durante's nose was colossal.
> The crowd was tremendous.

# The Encyclopedia

Having an encyclopedia in your home is like having a small library at your fingertips. It gives you access to information on topics in every field of knowledge. An encyclopedia is concerned with the who, what, when, where, how, and why of things. For example, an article on radar tells what radar is and who developed it, as well as when and where. It also describes how radar operates and why it is important in everyday life.

Most encyclopedias, whether they consist of one volume or more than one, are arranged alphabetically. They may have a single alphabetical arrangement from A through Z. Or they may also have a second alphabetical listing in the form of an index. The index will tell you which articles in the encyclopedia have information on the topic you are looking up. To make it even easier for you to find what you are looking for, some indexes refer you to the specific volume and page where the information appears.

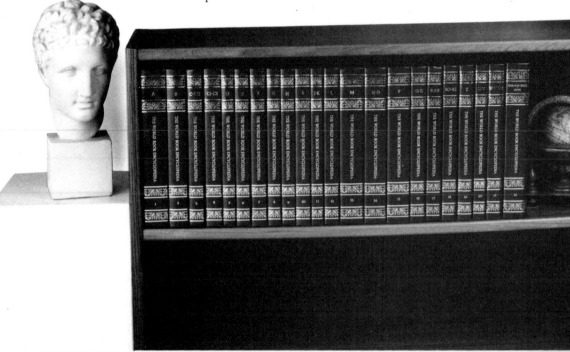

# The Computer in Your Home

If you are fortunate enough to have a computer in your home, don't think of it as just something on which you can play electronic video games. The computer can reduce your study time. With minimal programming skills or an appropriate commercial program, you will be able to use it to prepare for spelling, vocabulary, and math quizzes and tests. There are also a great number of math programs that drill, tutor, or carry on a dialogue in which the computer makes up problems and you solve them. Computer-assisted instruction (CAI), which is commercially available, can actually teach you biology, history, foreign languages, and numerous other subjects. With CAI, the computer takes you through a lesson step-by-step until the subject matter has been mastered. At the end of the lesson, the computer judges your performance according to predetermined standards.

## Other Home Helpers

Other things around your home can also be helpful in your studying. Don't overlook the informative magazines that come into your home every month. They provide articles and pictures that are often a valuable source of information for written reports and speeches. It would be to your advantage to find a way to file old magazines so that you are able to locate specific information in them on short notice. Even the daily newspapers are very useful. Newspapers provide you with a record of current events, and they give you an impression of how people perceived events at the time they occurred. Letters to the editor and editorials give you reactions to events and articles.

## Television and Radio

Just turn on your television or radio and you will find far more than entertainment. You can get interesting ideas and collect information for your reports from these media. Every week there are a number of special programs on television. The sponsors of these specials often prepare supplementary materials to inform viewers about the subjects of the programs. These study guides and bibliographies may be requested from the television network.

## Maps and Globes

Almost every home has a map or two lying around somewhere. While road maps may help your family plan trips, you can also use them to follow news events in different parts of the country. These maps are mostly used to find the locations of places and roads. But they can answer many other questions about places, such as size, proximity to water, and elevation.

When you are studying geography and countries of the world in social studies, use a globe to get an accurate picture of the earth as a whole. Distances, areas, and directions can be observed on a globe without the distortion seen on flat maps. A globe shows the positions of land and oceans exactly as they are on the earth.

## Other Books at Home

Few students appreciate the wealth of reference materials that are in their own homes. An almanac, even if it isn't the most recent edition, contains a wealth of information. Consult it when you want facts and figures about such topics as government, history, geography, population, sports, wars, crops, industry, presidents, movies, and famous people. Thumb through an almanac to see all that it offers. Although you may only read the *Guinness Book of World Records* for fun, it can be helpful as a study tool, also.

Take the time now to walk around your home and see what other materials you can find that will be helpful in your studying. Don't forget to look at the titles of books that have been gathering dust on shelves for a long time. Now is the time to find out what useful information might be in your brother's, sister's, or parents' old textbooks and reference books. Be imaginative in finding and using the study aids that are already in your own home.

## Visit the Library

Don't panic when you are given an assignment to make a speech or write a report on a topic that you have never even heard of. Your school or local library will almost surely have enough information on any topic to meet your needs. To many students, visiting the library is like visiting a foreign and forbidden land. They simply are not aware of the many resources and aids that a library offers. Whether you are continually faced with the task of doing research in the library or if you are just starting to do research there, the first place that you need to become acquainted with is the reference area. It contains a number of special books that you will find helpful. Reference books are not designed to be read from cover to cover. They are to be consulted for items of information on almost any topic. Books in this section will also tell you where else you should look in the library for more information.

## Choosing a Reference Book

*Think of reference books as tools. You want to find the tool that is designed for the job that you have to do.*

Think of reference books as tools. You want to find the tool that is designed for the job you have to do. Just as there are bread knives for slicing bread and steak knives for cutting meat, there are special reference books for particular kinds of information. Although you might find the correct spelling of a noun in the index of an encyclopedia, you would find it more quickly in a dictionary. Some facts about an elephant may be found in a dictionary, but an encyclopedia article is a more complete source of information. It would probably not be efficient to use a general encyclopedia to find out who holds the record for most major league strikeouts. Information such as this is much more easily found in an almanac.

Each type of reference book is designed to give you quick access to certain kinds of information. The following table will help you know which books to use:

| Information Needed | Reference Book |
| --- | --- |
| words | dictionary |
| general information | encyclopedia |
| geographical information | atlas (for maps) |
| | gazetteer (for facts) |
| statistical information | almanac |
| "how-to" information | handbook |
| people | biographical dictionary |
| names and addresses | directory |
| books and materials | bibliography |

You will find that some reference books cover many fields of knowledge, while others are very specialized and cover one field in depth. Browsing along the shelves of the reference section and examining the specialized reference tools available will help you become better acquainted with the many different books in this part of the library.

## More About Dictionaries

If you really want to go to the most comprehensive and authoritative dictionary in the English language, look for *The Oxford Dictionary of English Etymology.* You will be amazed at all the information that this reference tool supplies. It is an unabridged dictionary of several volumes.

Other unabridged dictionaries are usually found in one large volume. They are the dictionaries that you see sitting on their own stands in the library. Unabridged dictionaries contain almost all the words in the English language. Besides providing you with the definition, the pronunciation, and the origin and history of each word, these dictionaries also have biographical and geographical information, tables of measurements, abbreviations, and famous quotations. They also sometimes contain basic information about colleges, states, Presidents of the United States, and a wide variety of other facts.

The reference section of the library also has many specialized dictionaries. There are dictionaries that tell you how to use words, dictionaries that give you the oldest meaning of a word, and dictionaries that define words as they are used rather than how they should be used. A rhyming dictionary will help you get a poem written for literature class. The thesaurus will help you substitute new words for all the overused words in your writing. Science dictionaries give you technical terms for biology, chemistry, and physics. Chronologies and dictionaries of world history have short entries that cover people, events, and cultural trends.

If you want to know more about people like Pericles, Marie Antoinette, or John F. Kennedy, use a biographical dictionary. You will find short articles about men and women whose lives are important to the understanding of history. Music dictionaries cover compositions of music, musical performances, famous composers, abbreviations, forms of music, and instruments.

As a study aid for your literature class, there are dictionaries of American and English literature that give information about authors and their works. There are even dictionaries in which you can look up slang. These are often very readable and witty books, explaining grammar and rhetoric, word usage, literary concepts, clichés, phrases, idioms, and figures of speech.

Make sure you look in the front of any dictionary that you plan to use in order to find out what information the dictionary contains and how it is organized. Also check the key to abbreviations, codes, and symbols for each dictionary. Their meanings often vary from one dictionary to another.

## More About Encyclopedias

*An encyclopedia should be one of the first places you look when you are working on a report.*

When you need to know about Timbuktu, the state bird of Texas, or the first airplane ever built, go first to a general encyclopedia. In fact, an encyclopedia should be one of the first places you look when you are working on a report. Most reference sections of a library will contain several different sets of encyclopedias. Take the time to check the copyright date of any encyclopedia that you are using. Most encyclopedias have yearbooks that keep each set up to date. If you are looking for an event that happened recently, you might want to start with the yearbook.

Just like there are all kinds of dictionaries, there are many specialized encyclopedias. There are encyclopedias on technology, science, wildlife, pop and rock music, and space, to name just a few. There is even a set of encyclopedias on baseball that includes records of the yearly performances of batters, pitchers, fielders, managers, and teams. And if you need to know how to play cricket or boccie, you can go to the *Encyclopedia of All the Sports of the World*. Inside this encyclopedia, you will find explanations and rules for more than 230 sports.

## Atlases

When you want to know the distance from New York City to San Francisco, or the highest mountain in Asia, the reference book you need is an atlas—a book of maps. Sometimes it includes facts and figures about places. Geographical atlases usually contain charts, tables, and maps that show cities, towns, roads, countries, rivers, and mountains. They also show the size and relationships of land and water areas and the names of features and places. An index lists the names of such features and tells where to find them on the maps. The maps may also show the distribution of many other things, such as economic resources, population, types of climate, and plant life.

Some atlases include postal information and lists of national parks and monuments. Several countries publish atlases that have maps showing the physical, economic, and cultural resources of their nation in great detail.

## Almanacs

If you need to know who the fifth President of the United States was or how many barrels of oil were produced in Saudi Arabia last year, use an almanac. Almanacs are books that are published once a year. They are filled with all kinds of information, such as outstanding dates and events, short histories of countries and states, the movements of heavenly bodies, and facts about governments, history, geography, sports, and weather. They often also give figures on population, industry, and farm production.

### Other Reference Books

There are many other reference books in the library that you should know about and become familiar with. Acquaint yourself with *Current Biography,* a monthly publication that gives biographical information on people currently in the news. *Who's Who* tells about living American men and women and outstanding people in other countries. In the "how-to" category, there are many different reference works dealing with such topics as home repairs, gardening, and construction. Names and addresses can be found in all directories of professions and associations and also in telephone directories from various cities. Finally, there are bibliographies of all kinds, listing titles of books on various subjects and categories of subjects. Take the time to visit the reference area of your library. Ask the librarian to help you become familiar with the wealth of materials that are available.

### Cautions About Using Reference Works

As you begin to use reference books, you may be startled to learn that the facts in one book may not agree with the facts in another. Basic facts, such as the area of a country, may not be the same in two encyclopedias. When you encounter this problem, consult a third source. This may solve the problem. When information varies, be sure to identify your source. You may say, "According to Encyclopedia X, the elephant may grow to be 10 feet tall."

When you are looking for recent statistics, always check the date of the reference work. An almanac, for example, will contain facts from the year before the date appearing on the cover. An almanac for 1986 will cover the events up to and including the year 1985.

The same holds true for encyclopedias. Some encyclopedias undergo annual revision of substantial portions.

*When you are looking for recent statistics, always check the date of the reference work.*

Others go for years with little or no revision. Facts, maps, and other information can quickly go out of date. Get in the habit of checking copyright dates. The most recent date on the copyright page will indicate the year in which the volume was published.

## Library Organizations

Libraries give you access to the world's accumulated knowledge in many different forms, from books and magazines to microfilms and tapes. These materials are arranged so you can find them quickly, provided you understand how the materials are organized.

Most school and public libraries arrange and classify books according to Dewey Decimal Classification. Most college, university, and research libraries arrange and classify books according to Library of Congress Classification. Both systems are easy to use.

It is fairly easy to find out what is in a library. Most libraries have a catalog of their collection that often also includes such nonbook items as records, filmstrips, and documents. Just as the index to a book indicates which subjects are covered and on what pages information can be found, the library catalog lists the books and other materials in the library and tells where they are located. Once this information was found only on cards that were filed in alphabetical order in trays or drawers. This collection of cards is known as a card catalog. But now, more and more libraries are storing this information in computers that you must learn to operate in order to find materials in the library.

## Other Sources of Useful Information

Besides the card catalog, a library has a great many other sources of information that you can use in your research. One tool you should direct your attention to is *The Reader's Guide to Periodical Literature*. This source, which originated in the early 1900's, is the most up-to-date and complete assembly of articles in selected major magazines. The

*Readers' Guide* does not list every article published in every magazine, but it lists enough to satisfy most researchers. No library will have all the materials listed in the *Readers' Guide,* but many libraries can get almost any magazine or journal on loan from other libraries through the interlibrary loan system.

## Newspapers

Newspapers are excellent for current events. Most of the stories that are printed in newspapers never become available in book form. Most libraries have one or more local newspapers available on microfilm or in their original format. One newspaper, the *New York Times,* gives very complete coverage to the news and is very thoroughly indexed, making it a valuable research tool. In addition, the *New York Times Index* can be used to get the date a story occurred, so that you can track the story down in a local paper. Back files of newspapers are often photographed and kept on rolls of microfilm.

## The Vertical File

A library's vertical file is found in one or more filing cabinets. It has pamphlets, clippings, pictures, and other current materials that are difficult to store on a shelf. In a typical vertical file, you find folders of materials on such wide-ranging subjects as state senators, agriculture, space, health aids, Canada, cancer, and pollution. And these materials can usually be checked out.

## Records, Films, and Tapes

*If your library does not have the material you want, it can probably be borrowed from another library for you.*

Libraries have collections of records, films, filmstrips, and video cassettes. They also have microfiche editions of some books that are too rare or too expensive for the library to own in book form. The library may have a film or filmstrip that describes a college that you wish to attend. If you need a government document, the library has a catalog that will help you find it. And if your library does not have the material you want, it can probably be borrowed from another library for you. If you are doing a special report on a very technical subject, try to get permission to do research in the library at a local college.

## Study Aids for Your Subjects

Studying is more than sitting down with a textbook and plowing through it until a lesson is completed. Each subject you take in school has different kinds of information that you have to learn. And for each subject, there are different aids that can make learning more efficient. Some of these aids may be materials you already have at home or can find at the library. But many are aids that you will have to make or buy. Your study sessions will be more productive if you use study aids that really help you. Choose the ones that work for you, even if they are not the ones everybody is using.

*Your study sessions will be more productive if you use study aids that really help you.*

There are extra study aids that publishers have designed for almost every one of their textbooks. To find out what aids are available for your textbooks, read the preface or section to the students. You may find that the science book that has been giving you difficulty has a study guide or an outline. If you need more practice in solving equations, your math book may have booklets with extra problems for you to solve. These aids are far superior to any general aids that you might buy at a bookstore because they give you help with the textbooks that you are actually using. If you don't know where to buy these materials, ask your teacher to help you track them down.

## Foreign Language Study Aids

Learning to read and write a foreign language—not to mention understanding and speaking it—is quite a task. And the older you get, the harder the task becomes. One of the greatest challenges is trying to memorize hundreds of new words. The best aid for this job is flashcards.

Make your own flashcards by writing the foreign word on one side and the English equivalent on the other side. Or use a tape recorder to make an oral flashcard. Record an English word or a foreign language word. Then pause a few seconds before giving the equivalent word in the other language.

Back

Front

The longer you study a language, the greater the number of words you come across in your reading. You will need an English/foreign language dictionary so that you can look up the translations of words that you do not know.

Verbs, especially irregular verbs, seem to cause problems for many foreign language students. Verb wheels can help. With just a spin of the dial, a student can determine the correct forms of irregular verbs and regular ones, also. Ask your teacher to help you get verb wheels.

To speak a language, you need to become accustomed to hearing it. Find out if your textbook program has tapes that accompany it; most programs do. Also look at radio and television guides. Are there local broadcasts in the language that you are studying? At first, these programs may be impossible to understand. But with persistence, you will begin to recognize words, phrases, and even an occasional sentence. You will also begin to get a feel for the sound of the language.

*Probably the number-one study aid for math and science courses is the calculator.*

As you continue to study a language, you can increase your knowledge of it in so many different ways. Find a pen pal. Exchange books, magazines, newspapers, and records with this person. Better yet, explore the possibility of becoming an exchange student, or have one as a guest in your home.

## Math and Science Study Aids

Probably the number-one study aid for math and science courses is the calculator. Use it to ensure accuracy and speed in your calculations. Make sure your teacher approves the use of calculators for your assignments. Another aid to consider is flashcards. Use them to review the fundamentals of addition, subtraction, multiplication, and division. Also use them to learn the meanings of new words in science. Write the word on one side of the card and the meaning on the other side. Flashcards can also be used for learning equations and formulas that must be memorized.

Don't forget to investigate which additional study aids are available for your textbook. In addition, be sure you own a ruler that will measure customary and metric units, a protractor, and a compass. All these items will aid you in the study of math or science.

## English Study Aids

Whether you are in a sixth-grade English class or you are taking a college course in literature, you really need· to have a dictionary and a thesaurus in your study area. Since few students remember how to write footnotes or bibliographies, you will also need to have a style guide in order to write reports and term papers. Choose the one that your teacher recommends. Your textbook will probably answer all the questions you have about usage. But there are many books devoted to this subject if you need more sophisticated information.

If you have a computer with a printer and word-processing software, or access to one, use it to print out your papers. The computer lets you edit as you write and eliminates the need to rewrite or retype a paper—even if you need to write a second or third draft. Many computers have programs that check your spelling. They do not correct it; they only point out your errors. There are also grammar programs that will tell you if you have forgotten to begin a sentence with a capital letter or to finish it with an end mark. Again, the computer will not correct errors for you, but it will help point out some of your mistakes before you hand in your paper.

## Study Aids for Social Studies

History classes frequently call for memorizing many dates. Teachers may expect you to know such things as whether the Boer War was before or after World War I or whether Leonardo da Vinci painted the *Mona Lisa* or *The Last Supper* first. The easiest way to learn the sequence of events in history is to construct a time line for each chapter in your history textbook. If you use a roll of paper and leave considerable space between dates, you can easily add dates. Then you will have a useful aid when studying for tests, especially semester exams.

Other social studies aids that you might like to keep handy in your study area include a map of the United States, a map of the world, a globe, and a world atlas. The

*The easiest way to learn the sequence of events in history is to construct a time line for each chapter in your history textbook.*

latest almanac is helpful for statistics and quick facts about a country. You might also like to have an outline of the period of history you are studying. These outlines are available at most bookstores. Check with your teacher before buying one, and also be sure to find out what study aids accompany your textbook.

## Put Your Study Aids to Work

The list of study aids that you can use is very lengthy. What you need to do now is go to the library and become acquainted with the major materials in the reference section. Look at the unabridged dictionaries, encyclopedias, almanacs, and atlases. You need to know exactly what these books can offer you.

Don't use a study aid just because someone else does. Choose the study aids that really help you get the job done. Don't forget that your number-one helper is your textbook. Get to know every part of it. No other aid can come close in helping you study effectively.

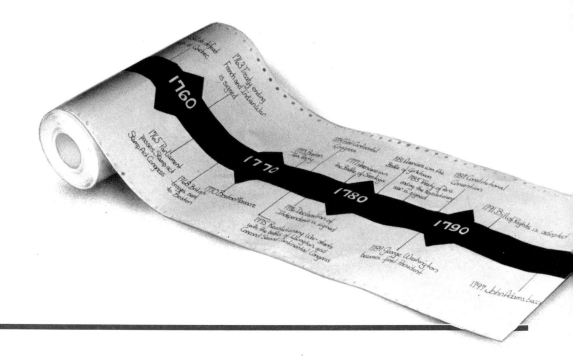

*Important study techniques that you should use are presented in this section.*

# The Best Way to Study

*M*any students do not know how to study. They may think that they do because they spend hours poring over textbooks trying to read every page in a chapter so that they can answer questions or prepare for a test. Is simply reading a chapter or a lesson the best way to study? Research shows that the average student learns less than half of the information he or she needs through simple reading of a homework assignment.

What, then, is the best way to study? There are many different ways of studying. The most effective way for any student depends greatly on how that student learns best. Consider the following questions carefully, for your answers will tell you more about what your learning style is:

1.  When you study hard for tests and receive good grades, do you—

    a.  study alone?

    b.  study with one or two friends?

    c.  study with a group of friends?

    d.  study alone sometimes and at other times with friends?

2.  When you learn new material easily, do you—

    a.  read the material?

    b.  write the material?

    c.  hear the material?

    d.  do some combination of reading, writing, and hearing the material?

3.  When you have an assignment for a class, do you—

    a.  prefer for someone to tell you exactly what to do?

    b.  prefer some direction from another person?

    c.  prefer to do the assignment without any
        direction?

    d.  prefer direction, some direction, or no direction
        depending on the assignment?

4. When you have the opportunity to learn new
   materials, do you—

    a.  enjoy learning the materials?

    b.  only enjoy learning the materials that you like?

    c.  occasionally enjoy learning the materials?

    d.  never enjoy learning the materials?

5. When you have homework assigned, do you—

    a.  complete the entire assignment?

    b.  complete the assignment when it was easy or
        interesting?

    c.  complete part of the assignment?

    d.  never complete the assignment?


# Your Learning Style

Now that you have answered these questions about the
ways you learn best, take the time to actually write down a
brief description of your learning style. You might write
something like this:

> I learn best when I study alone and write notes as I read.
> I also like the teacher to explain exactly what is to be
> learned. I usually enjoy learning new materials and I
> almost always complete the entire assignment because I
> like to stick with a task until it is done.

Note what a good picture this student has about personal
learning habits. This student would have an even clearer
picture by describing the lighting, heating, noise level, and
room arrangement that are preferable. This student could

also make note of favorite study positions and times of day best for studying. If this student has any peculiar habits, such as eating dry cereal or wearing a bathrobe while studying, they should be included in the description of learning style.

After you have some idea of how you learn best, it is time for you to learn more about study methods that you should use when you are in your prime studying atmosphere. Using these well-tested methods will make your study sessions both more efficient and shorter, as you learn how to condense material to a manageable quantity of information that is easy to remember. No longer will you stare at material, trying in vain to memorize and learn it. You will have methods such as outlining, underlining, note taking, and SQ3R to help you organize your learning. Let's take a look at these study methods and see how they can be put to work for you.

## Making Outlines

*Making an outline organizes your thinking. It forces you to discover what the main ideas of a topic are and how they are related to each other.*

Making an outline organizes your thinking. It forces you to discover what the main ideas of a topic are and how they are related to each other. It also shows what facts support each idea. Later on, when you use your outline to study for a test, you will not waste time trying to learn unimportant details. You will have an easy-to-read summary of a topic with the major points briefly listed for your review.

Outlines are made according to a standard form. The following example shows how you should organize an outline:

### Title

I. First main idea of the topic you are outlining

    A. Subtopic supporting this idea

        1. Important fact relating to A

            a. Detail supporting 1

      b.   Second detail supporting 1

         (1) Minor detail supporting b

            (a) Item supporting (1)

            (b) Another item supporting (1)

         (2) Another item supporting b

    2.   Another important fact relating to A

  B.  Another subtopic supporting the first main idea

    1.   Important fact relating to B

    2.   Another important fact relating to B

II. Second main idea of the topic you are outlining

  A.  Subtopic

  B.  Subtopic

  C.  Subtopic

III. Third main idea of the topic you are outlining

  A.  Subtopic

  B.  Subtopic

Note that there are always two or more headings supporting each subdivision and that the different subdivisions are indented to show their relative importance. How detailed you make a study outline depends on the topic you are outlining as well as the purpose of your outline. Be careful not to make your study outline so detailed that it stops being an outline and becomes a lengthy summary that takes a long time to read and digest.

    You can write the various headings of your outline in phrases or short sentences. Sometimes, minor headings don't need to be more than just a word. The order of the points on your outline should be in some logical pattern. Outlines often have a chronological, or time, order in which items are listed from earliest to latest dates. Another logical arrangement is by size or quantity, going from largest to smallest or vice versa. When it comes to outlining a book or speech, you should follow the author's or speaker's subdivisions of chapters, topics, or main points.

## Looking at Outlines

You can find many excellent examples of outlines in encyclopedias. Look at this outline from an encyclopedia article on leaves. Note how all the main ideas are tied together and how easy it is to distinguish between the main ideas and the subtopics.

**Leaves**

I.  The importance of leaves

II. The life story of a leaf
    A.  A leaf begins its life
    B.  The leaf becomes fully grown
    C.  The leaf changes color
    D.  The leaf dies

III. The parts of a leaf
    A.  The blade
    B.  The petiole
    C.  The stipules

IV. How a leaf makes food
    A.  Obtaining the raw materials
    B.  Photosynthesis
    C.  Transpiration

V.  Specialized leaves
    A.  Protective leaves
    B.  Storage leaves
    C.  Tendrils
    D.  Bracts
    E.  Insect-capturing leaves

VI. How to collect leaves

    A.  How to preserve leaves

    B.  How to make leaf rubbings and prints

Don't you think the above outline, with some added detail under each subtopic, would have been helpful if you were reviewing for a test or writing a paper on leaves? You probably would not have to reread the original material if you outlined the material properly.

## Testing Your Ability to Outline

Suppose you are writing a term paper on the pollution of Lake Michigan, and you have compiled the following list of important ideas. How would you arrange them into an outline that shows the main ideas (I, II, etc.) and subtopics (A, B, etc.)?

### The Pollution of Lake Michigan

*Thesis sentence:* Because Lake Michigan is extensively polluted, only strong laws will provide an effective solution.

The causes of pollution
Sewage treatment regulations
Solutions to the problem
Pesticides used for farming
Increased cost of water purification
Undesirable levels of algae
Evidence of pollution
Industrial wastes
Maximum water temperature regulation
Thermal pollution from nuclear energy plants
Pesticide controls
Contaminated fish
Inadequately treated sewage
Laws limiting industrial emissions

Once you have finished writing an outline based on this list, take the time to check and see how you did. The following is the most logical and consistent outline of the data as given. Note that the subtopics (A, B, etc.) could be given in any order.

I. Evidence of pollution
   A. Contaminated fish
   B. Increased cost of water purification
   C. Undesirable levels of algae

II. The causes of pollution
   A. Industrial wastes
   B. Pesticides used for farming
   C. Inadequately treated sewage
   D. Thermal pollution from nuclear energy plants

III. Solutions to the problem
   A. Laws limiting industrial emissions
   B. Pesticide controls
   C. Sewage treatment regulations
   D. Maximum water temperature regulation.

*The secret to good outlining is finding the main ideas and relating them to one another properly.*

The secret to good outlining is finding the main ideas and relating them to one another properly. The more outlines you make, the better your outlines will become, so get into the habit of outlining material whenever you study.

## Underlining

When you are studying a book or magazine, you can underline key words, phrases, and sentences in order to identify the facts and ideas you wish to remember. Obviously, this is only possible when you own the material. The biggest mistake that students make is underlining too much.

You should read a passage, think about it, and then go back and underline the key points. If underlining is done thoughtfully, you can reread the underlined parts for a good review of important facts and ideas. To underline, use a colored pencil or a special marker that highlights. Avoid using colored pens and ordinary markers. They tend to be messy, since they often bleed through a page.

The material you choose to underline depends greatly on the reason you have for underlining it. Observe how easy it is to capture the main points of the following article on whales by just reading the underlined parts. You would underline this article quite differently if your major concern was the size of the animals rather than just learning basic facts about whales.

A whale is a <u>huge sea animal</u> that looks much like a fish. But <u>whales are not fish</u>. They belong instead to the <u>group of animals called mammals</u>. Other mammals include chimpanzees, dogs, and human beings. Like the mammals, whales have a <u>highly developed brain</u> and so are <u>among the most intelligent of all animals</u>.

Most whales are enormous creatures. One kind, the <u>blue whale, is the largest animal that has ever lived</u>. Blue whales may grow up to 100 feet (30 meters) long and weigh more than 100 short tons (91 metric tons). However, <u>some kinds of whales are much smaller</u>. Belugas and narwhals, for example, grow only 10 to 15 feet (3 to 5 meters) long.

Underlining does not need to be limited to books and magazines. Many students find it helpful to underline key points or facts in their outlines or notes in order to prepare for tests. This helps to reduce the amount of material that must be reviewed prior to exam time.

## Taking Notes

Notes are important, especially good notes. They serve as reminders that will help you with your studying. There is much more to note taking than just writing things down. In order to take good notes, you must first carefully read your textbook assignments or listen attentively to your class lectures. Keep in mind that taking notes from your textbook involves different skills than taking notes in your classroom.

For either type of note taking, though, it is not advisable to use single sheets of note paper. Single sheets of paper can be too easily lost. It is best to select a loose-leaf notebook containing lined note paper. The best paper size is usually 8½ inches by 11 inches. This size provides you with enough room so that you will be able to take legible notes. If there is a need for additional pages, these can be inserted. A spiral-bound notebook does not give you the same flexibility to rearrange your notes.

It is important to take the time to organize your loose-leaf notebook. You should have dividers between each subject. Each divider should have a tab that sticks out and displays the name of that subject. It is a good idea to have one section of your notebook set aside for recording your homework assignments. Include your study calendar in this section, and be sure that you mark all assignments on the calendar so that you will allow enough time to plan and complete long-range assignments.

*In order for notes to be most meaningful, they must be expressed in your own words.*

## Short Cuts in Taking Notes

Don't copy straight out of your textbook. You will have to write too much, and in order for notes to be most meaningful, they need to be expressed in your own words. Develop your own short cuts. Skip unnecessary words, and do not worry about grammar. Drop suffixes like *-tion* and *-ing*. You can also improve your note-taking skills by using standard abbreviations and symbols. You will write your notes even faster if you don't use periods with the abbreviations. Look at the following list showing some sample abbreviations and symbols:

| **Abbreviations** | | **Symbols** | |
|---|---|---|---|
| AM | before noon | & | and |
| Cong | congress | = | equals |
| E | east | $ | dollars |
| eg | for example | % | per cent |
| etc | and so forth | ? | question |
| sig | signature | < | less than |
| st | street | + | plus |
| US | United States | $H_2O$ | water |

Take a minute and see if you can think of at least five abbreviations or symbols to add to the list. In some encyclopedia sets, you can find several pages of standard abbreviations in an article entitled "Abbreviation." See how many of these abbreviations are familiar to you, and try to remember others for future use.

It is a good idea to create your own form of shorthand for note taking. Begin by shortening one or two words that you frequently use in taking notes. Add a few words to your list each week. Before long, you will have your own note-taking system. You must remember to make your abbreviations clear enough so that they will not be mistaken for other words. Can you identify each of the following abbreviations? The vowels have been left out of each word.

| | |
|---|---|
| pplr | popular |
| hmsphr | hemisphere |
| tmbr | timber |
| cttl | cattle |
| qn | queen |

Another way to shorten words is to use the beginning letters of a word to stand for the word. For example:

| | |
|---|---|
| add | address |
| biol | biology |
| soc st | social studies |
| math | mathematics |
| sci | science |

Long words are usually easier to abbreviate than short words. Keep in mind that the reason you are using abbreviations and symbols is to make note taking quicker and easier. Choose short cuts that are simple to remember. Then get in the habit of using these short cuts.

## Textbook Notes

Many students who own their textbooks do underlining and note taking right in the book. But most students cannot, since they are only renting the books. Therefore, they take notes. Keep in mind that note taking is a personal matter, so your notes will probably not look like anyone else's. Some students like to write down very detailed notes, while others prefer to keep their notes briefly in a list or in outline form. Some students think that it takes longer to write textbook notes in an outline form, but after you get in the habit, you will be able to do it just as fast as other methods. Remember that if you use the textbook headings and subheadings for your outline, you will have the skeleton of your notes completed before you even begin taking notes.

*If you use the textbook headings and subheadings for your outline, you will have the skeleton of your notes completed before you even begin.*

## Notes for Reports

When you are taking notes for a report or a term paper, you need to be more systematic and careful than when you are taking notes in class or from your textbook. This is because you will be reading and gathering information from many different sources. For this reason, it is a good idea to use 3" × 5" note cards. If they are too small, use 4" × 6" cards. The cards can be shuffled around more easily than sheets of paper, making it easier to organize your paper. At the top of each card, make sure you put down such information as source, author, and page number. Do not start writing a paper and end up not being able to include key quotes or facts because you do not remember the sources.

Always read your sources thoroughly before you start taking notes. Be very selective. Do not copy unimportant details or parts you think you can easily remember. Write only summary sentences or factual material, such as statistics, that will be important to your report or term paper. If you are going to use a direct quote, make sure you copy it word-for-word and remember to use quotation marks. Do not rewrite a quote in your own words. However, if you decide to leave out part of a quotation, write three spaced dots (. . .), called an ellipsis, to show where words or sentences were left out.

Put each new idea on a separate card. Your cards will be easier to rearrange and organize later, when you begin to draft your paper. Also be sure to put information from different sources on separate cards, even if they say the same thing about the same subject.

## Taking Notes in Class

In order to take good notes in the classroom, you have to be a good listener. This means that you will need to be able to concentrate on what your teacher is saying, identify what the major points are, decide what is important, and quickly record these facts in your notebook in a well-organized way. You should be able to sift out all unnecessary information and block out all other noises. If you feel that you are a poor listener, try a few of the following activities to improve your listening skills:

1. Listen carefully to a news report on the radio. When the program is over, write down all the major news items that were spoken about in the broadcast.

2. Take notes during a club meeting. When the meeting is over, check your notes with the secretary of the club to see how your notes compare.

3. Play a listening game with your friends. For example, say: "I am going on a trip and I'm going to take . . ." Each person names an item and also repeats the items the other players gave.

> *The classroom lecture is one of the most important learning situations in which you participate.*

The classroom lecture is one of the most important learning situations in which you participate. This is the time when you discover exactly what your teacher expects you to know. Yet, many students fail to take classroom lectures seriously. Answer the following questions "Yes" or "No" to see what kind of a listener you are:

1. Do I listen aggressively, concentrate on the teacher's words, and stay on the alert for major points?

2. Do I sit in the back of the room or near a door or window where distractions may occur?

3. Am I able to avoid emotional reactions to the teacher's statements, reactions that could block learning?

4. Do I listen for word cues from the teacher that indicate important ideas?

5. Am I always ready to ask questions when some point of information needs to be clarified?

6. Do I use lined note paper in a loose-leaf binder as my notebook?

7. Do I study my assignment before the lecture?

8. Have I developed my own shorthand to improve note-taking speed?

9. Do I try to take down every word my teacher says?

10. Am I careful to write down any examples my teacher may use to clarify points?

11. Do I carefully review my lecture notes?

All of your answers except 2. and 9. should be "Yes." Each incorrect answer may indicate a deficiency in listening skills that could affect your success in the classroom.

## Classroom Listening Secrets

Sit in the front or center of the classroom. Sitting in the back of the room or near a door or window will hurt your concentration. Too many distractions may occur. The result may also be that you will not hear what your teacher is saying. Sitting in the front or center of the room will enable you to hear better. It will also enable you to clearly see materials written on the blackboard.

Avoid emotional reactions that might block learning. Good listeners are aware of this problem. Poor listeners will tune the teacher off the moment they hear an idea with which they do not agree. Try to concentrate on what is being said rather than reacting with agreement or disagreement to the lecture.

Listen for cues that indicate important ideas. Writing down every word your teacher says is time consuming, and it usually clutters up your notes with insignificant details. Listen carefully for cues that indicate important ideas. Does your teacher use a voice inflection to make a point stand out? Does you teacher use a topic sentence and a summary statement? Does your teacher indicate a number of important subpoints by cue statements such as "the three reasons . . ." or "a list of five . . ."? Does your teacher repeat important statements, or say things like, "Listen carefully to this point"? All of these cues will help you in recording important ideas in your notes.

*Listen for cues that indicate important ideas.*

Be ready to ask questions. Sometimes your teacher will set aside time for a discussion period. This is the time to ask questions that will help you clear up anything you missed in the lecture.

## Taking Lecture Notes

Class lectures become important in high school and even more so in college. In junior high and elementary school, it is also important to take notes on what the teacher says.

You must have good listening and note-taking skills to do well in lecture classes. Study your assignment before the lecture. At the conclusion of a lecture, your teacher will probably announce the topic for the next lecture. Study the related textbook materials before the lecture. This will enable you to have a good background of the ideas to be presented by your teacher. The lecture will become more meaningful, and you will also be in a better frame of mind to take good notes.

Learn to take notes in outline form. You cannot take down every word your teacher says. Therefore, you must learn how to prepare an outline. As you listen, your notes should only include the important ideas. Good notes are an outline and not a word-for-word record of a lecture.

Write down the examples given in a lecture. Your teacher will probably use examples to clarify particular points. Include the examples in your notes. They will help you gain a greater understanding of the main idea.

*Notes should be reviewed and reorganized the same day they are taken.*

Review your lecture notes. Most notes need editing to put them into the most useful form. Well-organized notes will improve your ability to remember these materials. Notes should be reviewed and reorganized the same day they are taken.

## SQ3R

Many research studies have been done to help students learn how to study more efficiently. One of these studies resulted in a method for study that has been used successfully by many students. This method is called the SQ3R method. SQ3R stands for *s*urvey, *q*uestion, and (3R's) *r*ead, *r*ecite, and *r*eview, which are the steps that students follow when they use this method of study. It is really worth taking the time to try this method if you never have. SQ3R works especially well when applied to the study of a textbook. So, the next time you have to study a chapter in your science or social studies textbook, give SQ3R a try.

## Survey

You start with the letter *S*, which stands for *survey*. This means you must begin by reading all the headings and sub-headings in the assigned material. Textbooks are written from well-organized outlines. The main points of an out-line are usually used as headings in a textbook. Headings are important clues to the contents of a chapter. In addi-tion, if a summary is available, read this as part of your survey of a chapter. A survey of the headings and the sum-mary will give you most of the important ideas in a chap-ter. The number of headings and subheadings will vary from book to book. However many or few there are, they represent the framework on which the textbook has been written.

These features introduce the material to be learned. For example, in a chapter dealing with the Revolutionary War in America, these headings might appear:

The Causes of the War

Events Leading to the Revolution

The First Battles

These headings alert you to what the general information in the chapter will be. As soon as you have read them, you know that the chapter will deal with causes of the war, events before the war, and the first battles of the war. In other words, you know quite a bit about the chapter with-out even reading it.

## Question

After you have carefully surveyed the material, you need to change all the headings in the chapter into questions. Questions help you learn, because they make you think about what it is that you are studying. Questions challenge you and give you a purpose for your learning.

This technique may be difficult for you if you have not done it in the past. But with practice, you will find that it grows easier to ask yourself questions. For example, in the chapter dealing with the Revolutionary War, you need to change the headings into questions. Such questions might be:

What were the main causes of the Revolutionary War?

What was happening in America before the Revolutionary War?

What were the names of the first battles?

These questions serve as a broad guide to study. You will find that questions usually tip you off to what the textbook writer considers to be the important information. Under each of the headings, subheadings often appear. For example:

The first battles

Men under arms

War leaders

Battlefronts

You should turn these subheadings into questions, also:

Who were the soldiers who fought in the war?

Who were the war leaders of each side?

Where were the first battles fought?

*Questions usually tip you off to what the textbook writer considers to be the important information.*

Make a written list of all your questions, and keep them in the same order that the headings appear in the textbook. Be sure to leave enough space on your paper after each question so that you can write an answer for it later. Keep all these questions in a notebook. With a framework of questions now written down, you are ready to go on to the next step.

## Read

Read the textbook. Read thoroughly and carefully in order to answer all your questions. Make sure that you understand what you are reading. Read everything, including captions, charts, graphs, and activities. Everything in a textbook has some purpose. Be thorough in your reading. Remember that any information worth an illustration is probably quite important.

As you read, you should look up unfamiliar words in a dictionary. If you find that looking up words breaks your concentration, then make a list of the unfamiliar words and look them up when you have finished reading. Unfamiliar words that are essential to the meaning of a passage, though, must be looked up right away.

The meanings of some words become clear from the context in which they are used. For example, a reader might catch the meaning of a word such as *divinity* from a previous phrase *all-powerful single god*. In any case, you should master the meaning of all the words in an assignment in order to fully understand the assignment.

## Recite

Once you have read a section, stop and repeat aloud the major ideas under each heading. Do this without looking at the book. Then answer the questions for the section in your own words, and give examples when necessary. If you succeed, write down the answers in your notebook and then go on and read the next section. If you fail, go back, reread the section, and try to answer the questions again. When you are ready for the next section, repeat the process: read to answer the questions, then look away from the book and recite the answers to the questions before writing the answers. Continue this procedure until you have completed the entire assignment.

*Once you have read a section, stop and repeat aloud the major ideas under each heading.*

If a particular subject or chapter in a textbook is extremely difficult for you, take the time to construct an outline using the most important ideas you are able to find in each paragraph. The framework for such an outline should be drawn from the list of basic questions you constructed earlier. Such an outline might look something like this:

I. Causes of the war

    A. Political conflicts

        1. Wanted control of local affairs

        2. Also wanted respect of the British government

    B. Economic rivalry

        1. British laws controlled trade

        2. British government tried to slow expansion to the West

        3. British government controlled trade with the Indians.

This extra effort will help you remember important details that may be giving you difficulty.

## Review

*Reviewing should take place immediately after you have completed the first four steps in the SQ3R method.*

You are now at the final step of SQ3R. You are ready to go back over the material and review it. Survey again what you have read. Skim over the headings of the chapter, ask yourself what they mean and what information they contain. Recite the important ideas under each heading. Answer the question you made earlier for each heading. Reread if you cannot answer the question without looking at the textbook. Your review should include studying an outline, if you have one.

Finally, you should complete any activities and answer any end-of-chapter questions contained in your textbook. Remember to also review any class notes at this time. All of this written material should be kept carefully filed for future reviews. The material will be very helpful later when you must prepare for tests.

Reviewing is not something that you should do only at the end of a chapter or before taking an examination. It should take place immediately after you have completed the first four steps in the SQ3R method.

## Reasons for SQ3R

The SQ3R method might seem like a slow and laborious way to grasp the meaning of an assignment. It is. But it is also a tried-and-true method to understanding what you read, and it has worked for many people. You will find that the more you use the method, the easier it becomes. Questions gradually become easier to create. You begin to recognize key points and ideas more quickly. Reading becomes more concentrated, and information is absorbed more easily.

When you decide to try this method, however, remember that you must be patient. Results over a short range of time will not be great. But if you make an honest effort to apply the SQ3R method, the long-range payoff will be substantial. Keep in mind that using this method should also help you learn to read faster, pick out important points in your reading more quickly, and fix these points more readily in your memory. Examination questions may also seem more familiar, because headings turned into questions are often the points that teachers emphasize in tests.

## Studying for Each Subject

Each subject you take in school has different kinds of information that you have to learn. Because of this, you must approach the study of each subject in a slightly different way. You cannot study mathematics the same way that you study social studies. Practicing your tennis serve will help improve your skills for gym class, but it will do nothing to improve your writing skills in English. You need to know what special kind of study skills are necessary for each class in order to succeed at school.

Each subject also has its own unique vocabulary that must be mastered. For example, in science you will need to know such words as *chlorophyll, evaporation,* and *gravity,* while in mathematics there are technical terms like *factor, associative property,* and *divisor.* There are even complications of words, like *product,* which mean different things in different subjects. For each subject, you must devise a method to learn the vocabulary. Many students find that the best way to learn terms is to make flashcards.

What follows are some suggestions for the most efficient ways to study various subjects. If you put these suggestions to practice, your performance in school should improve.

## Social Studies

When your assignment calls for a chapter to be read in your social studies book, you should familiarize yourself with the pages before you ever read the first word. Glance over all the pages in the assigned chapter to see what is on each page. Look at the pictures, maps, charts, and graphs. These will help you to get a clearer picture of what the author is writing about. Then read the textbook. In other words, use SQ3R, which is probably the best method for studying social studies. If you don't want to use the question part of SQ3R, you should either outline or take notes on what you have read.

After you have finished reading a chapter, make sure that you take the time to do any end-of-chapter exercises. These exercises give you the opportunity to test yourself and to see if you can apply the concepts that you have learned.

## Mathematics

*Mathematics is a subject that must be studied daily. Don't let yourself fall behind.*

Mathematics is a subject that must be studied daily. Don't let yourself fall behind. You must keep up with your class. Math is a cumulative subject, which means that what you learn one week is a building block for what you are going to learn the following week.

Most all the work you do in math class involves solving problems. You will be better prepared to do this work if you take notes in class and write down every example that your teacher shows on the blackboard. Carefully read a problem twice to determine what things are given, what principles and relationships are stated or implied, and what needs to be found or proven. Write down the essentials before you set up the problem. Concentrate on analyzing the problem first, and don't hurry into the computation. Sometimes you can draw a diagram that gives you a better picture of the facts, principles, and relationships. Then you are ready to apply your computational skills. Estimating your answer before you do your computation can be helpful. Be sure to take the time to check your answer and find out where you went wrong in your calculations if you made any mistakes.

## Science

Use the SQ3R method to study science. Reading ahead before class helps you feel at home with the unfamiliar words and concepts that you may meet in class. Like math, you must keep up with your daily work in your science class. Because the material is difficult, review your notes several times a week. Keep a record in your notebook of all the important formulas and principles. You may even wish to put them on note cards.

*Use the SQ3R method to study science.*

Many science classes also have a lab section that you are required to take. Be prepared when you walk into the lab to do your experiment. Know what you are expected to do and how you are going to do it. This means that you should read the lab manual and the appropriate sections of your textbook ahead of time.

## English Grammar and Composition

You need to know more than just the rules of English grammar; you must be able to apply them and do exercises for class. Always read a rule and its examples before writing out an exercise. And don't forget to correct your errors when you find out what the answers are. Use the grammar rules you learn in everything you write.

An inability to spell common words correctly quickly lowers your composition grades. Many words commonly misspelled are known as spelling demons. They are words that usually have an irregular arrangement of letters and require special study. Ask your teacher to help you obtain a list of such words, and study them until you can spell them accurately.

You should also obtain self-help tests for spelling. Such tests include lists of commonly misspelled words. Fill out some of the spelling tests, and check to see if you spelled all the words correctly. If you have errors, do the following:

1. Visualize each misspelled word in every detail.
2. Spell each word aloud.
3. Write each word out.
4. Check for difficult spots in each word.

Words are sometimes misspelled because they are mispronounced. Always be sure to check words in the dictionary when you are not sure of the correct pronunciation.

In English composition, these guidelines will help you to improve your writing:

1. Define your central theme clearly.
2. Develop an outline and follow it.
3. Keep in mind the principles of good composition (unity, coherence, emphasis, and adequate development).
4. Be concise.
5. Proofread your finished paper.
6. Do not be afraid to make revisions.
7. Check for spelling errors by reading your compositions backward, word-by-word. This method guarantees that you actually read each individual word.

*Be yourself when you write. Do not try to imitate someone else's style of writing.*

Most important, be yourself when you write. Do not try to imitate someone else's style of writing. If you are unsure of punctuation, grammar, or spelling, refer to your English composition book and a dictionary. You should keep these handy at all times.

## Foreign Languages

Studying a foreign language is rather complicated, since you are learning to speak, read, and write the language all at the same time. Like mathematics, foreign languages are cumulative subjects, so daily study is essential. Otherwise, what you don't learn one day will cause you trouble later on.

*Like mathematics, foreign languages are cumulative subjects, so daily study is essential.*

Much of your work in a foreign language consists of grammar exercises. Take notes when the teacher explains a new point of grammar, then read the rules in the textbook and study the examples before you begin the exercises. If you don't understand an exercise, be sure to ask questions until you do.

You will also be required to read material in the foreign language you are studying. Amounts of required reading will increase with each year you study the language. Try to read through a lesson without stopping to translate each new word, and simply try to grasp the general meaning of the selection. Then reread the selection, and make a flashcard for each word that you do not know. Practice with these cards often. As you master a word, remove it from your active set of cards and place it into your review set, which you should go through once a week.

You learn to speak a language by actually speaking it—not just by reading or writing it. So, after you read a story silently, read it aloud. After you do an exercise, read it aloud, also. Take five minutes each day to speak the foreign language aloud to yourself. Find a fellow student in your class with whom you can carry on conversations in the foreign language outside of class. Regular practice at speaking a foreign language is one of the best ways to gain fluency.

## Final Study Tips

Today's schools use many different kinds of study arrangements to help you succeed at school. You may find yourself working alone in a study carrel or studying with a larger group of students. Sometimes you may work with two or three students as a team. Be sure to always place yourself in the environment in which you study best. At home, you probably study alone, but there are times when group study with fellow students can be profitable.

How much you learn when studying by yourself depends on how well you use your study skills. Group studying succeeds only when you and your fellow students stick to studying. To make group studying valuable, each student should contribute to the discussion, raise questions, and make comments. Much can be done in group study to solve difficult problems, share knowledge, understand assignments, clarify ideas, and review for tests. Each student's ideas add to those of the others in the group, and this helps to increase everyone's understanding of a subject.

## Review, Review, Review

Within two hours of studying unfamiliar material, you can forget almost one-half of it. Even if you have a great memory, you can forget one-fourth or more of what you have learned in just one day. The best way to remember what you have studied is to keep reviewing it.

*The best way to remember what you have studied is to keep reviewing it.*

You must build review time into each study session. This explains why the last step of SQ3R is review. It is also a good reason for doing your homework regularly, because your homework is almost always a review of what you are learning in class.

The first time you must review new material is immediately after you have studied it. This should be a short review, since the material will still be rather fresh in your mind. Just go over your outline, notes, or questions, and tell yourself what you have learned. Later in the day or the next day, you should go over the material again. As you continue to learn more about a subject, go back and review once a week so that you retain a total picture of what you are learning. You can't just set aside your material to be reviewed, or soon you will be doing nothing but reviewing. So each time you review, reduce the size of your notes by underlining, outlining, or writing the most important facts on note cards. Then your review periods will not need to last more than ten to fifteen minutes, perhaps one-half hour for more difficult material. Sunday afternoon or evening is often a good time to schedule a weekly review session. You will also need to schedule special review sessions before taking tests.

## Studying for Tests

As a student, you probably feel as if you are always preparing for and taking tests. This activity is never very pleasant. But if you review new or difficult material frequently, you will not need to have a long cramming session before a test. What you need to do is to concentrate on things you don't know or aren't sure of. Only this material needs to be reread. A good way to find out what you know and don't know is to see if you can answer the questions you developed as part of the SQ3R study method or the questions at the end of a unit or chapter in a textbook. You also need to review the notes you made during lectures and class discussions.

*If you review new or difficult material frequently, you will not need to have a long cramming session before a test.*

One thing that you should do when studying for a test is to think about the types of tests your teacher likes to give. Some teachers prefer true-false, multiple-choice, and short-answer tests, which demand that you recall specific facts. Others like to give essay tests, in which you not only have to deal with facts but also state opinions and back them up with convincing information. Some teachers like to combine objective and essay questions. In any case, you should gear your studying to the kind of test you are likely to face. Don't forget to pay close attention to what the teacher says in class during the days before a test. What the teacher is saying often applies to what will be on the test. Remarks like "It is very important to know the causes of the Revolutionary War," and "We have studied the parts of the atom this six weeks," may be very strong clues to what will be on a test.

## Memory Tips

Quickly answer the following questions:

What is the title of this section?

What is the name of this volume?

What is the number of this volume?

Could you answer all of these questions? If not, perhaps it is because you are not interested in learning this information and you are not making an effort to learn it. It is often the same story with school—students learn what interests them and what they want to remember.

*Students learn what interests them and what they want to remember.*

If you want to remember, put time into a subject. As you begin to learn that subject, your interest in the subject will probably increase. Be sure to decide what you want to learn, because that is what you will learn. Here are a few additional tips that will help you improve your memory:

1.  Consider your learning style. If you learn when you write, then let your writing and note taking help you remember. If you learn when you recite, then read your notes aloud and discuss the subject with others. If you learn when you read, then read and reread the textbook, your notes, your outline, book summaries, and other materials. If you learn when you hear, then listen carefully in class and to discussions.

2.  Concentrate on the task. Center your attention on what you are trying to learn. Use all your willpower to stop your mind from wandering. Choose a study area that has a limited number of distractions.

3.  Remember by association. Try to associate what you are learning with what you know. If you already know three parts of a plant, then learn three more by relating them to the parts you already know.

4. Use memory devices. For remembering lists, like the names of U.S. Presidents or the order of the planets from the sun, try using abbreviations, word order, rhymes, silly sentences, and other memory aids. For example, the first letter of each of the names of the Great Lakes is found in the word *homes* or in the sentence "*H*er *o*rder *may embarrass Sally.*"

5. Space your learning. Instead of studying for two hours, memorize material in several short spurts of ten, fifteen, or twenty minutes.

## Study Skills Check List

Even if you are earning straight A's in school right now, you still may not be studying in the most effective way. See if you can honestly answer "Yes" to the following check list of questions:

1. Do you really know what your learning style is?

2. Can you write an outline using the correct form?

3. Do you identify the key words and phrases when you underline?

4. Do you write down only the key points when you take notes?

5. Are you using SQ3R to study for science and social studies classes?

6. Do you use different study methods for each subject?

7. Do you have a regular pattern for reviewing built into your study schedule?

8. Do you prepare for a test by making up and answering questions on the material to be tested?

9. Are you interested in learning how to study better?

10. Have you attached your own individual learning style to the methods that you use to study?

# VI HOW TO GET HELP WITH STUDY PROBLEMS

*There are many people who can help you solve your study problems, and this section tells you how to get help when you need it.*

DECEMBER

| S | M | T | W | T | F | S |
|---|---|---|---|---|---|---|
| | 1 | 2 | 3 | 4 | 5 | 6 |
| 7 | 8 | 9 | 10 | 11 | 12 | 13 |
| 14 | 15 | 16 | 17 | 18 | 19 | 20 |
| 21 | 22 | 23 | 24 | 25 | 26 | 27 |
| 28 | 29 | 30 | 31 | | | |

21 Winter begins
25 Christmas
26 Hanukkah
31 New Year's Eve

4 Election Day
11 Veterans Day
27 Thanksgiving Day

**THURSDAY**
**13**

Swim Meet

**FRIDAY**
**14**

English Quiz
Pep Rally

**SATURDAY**
**15**

**SUNDAY**

# How to Get Help with Study Problems

T here may be times when you find yourself falling behind in your work. You may still be working to finish one assignment when you are given another—then still another. With each new assignment, you fall further and further behind.

When this happens, you may become excited and panic. You may rush to finish the work quickly. Because you hurry, you make mistakes. So, the problem grows worse instead of better.

Other times, you may feel completely lost in a class. Perhaps everyone in your math class knows how to find the least common denominator. You don't even know the difference between the numerator and the denominator, and you don't have any idea of how to do the assignment.

So you sit, rather embarrassed, and stare at a blank piece of paper—only scribbling something down when the answers are put on the board. And then your teacher announces that you must know how to find the least common denominator if you are ever going to be able to subtract fractions. How do you react to this? Do you feel totally discouraged? Do you just give up trying to understand fractions?

Perhaps some kind of crisis is always occurring in your life that interferes with your studying. Are your parents getting a divorce? Has your best friend just been in a car accident? Was your hair ruined by the perm that your mother talked you into getting? These crises may make you so upset that you cannot study. You become unable to concentrate because you are always thinking of your problems.

Emotions can mix up your thoughts. It becomes difficult to think rationally. You become unsure of yourself. You get nervous and become more and more upset. It would be easy at this point to give up and do nothing.

But that is not the way to act when you have a problem at school. The worst thing to do is to give up. Nothing is gained by giving up. Instead, stop and think, "How can I get back on track with my studies?" Fortunately, there are a number of people that you can turn to when you need help.

## Talk with Your Teacher

You can expect your teachers to be available to help when you need it. Your teachers do not want you to fail. They want you to succeed. Most teachers are more than willing to listen and offer suggestions on how a school problem might be solved.

Be sure to talk to your teacher about problems with your studies before they become too serious. If you are having trouble understanding what the class is doing, you can probably talk to your teacher while the class is working on a written assignment. Your teacher may be able to help you immediately to understand the lesson. If speaking with your teacher during class is not possible, then you should arrange to have a conference.

## Having a Conference

If there is not enough time in class to get help, make an appointment to see your teacher before or after school or during a free or study period. Most teachers have a free period during the day that they set aside to work with students. Remember that your teacher is a busy person with many students to keep track of and help. Therefore, find a time when both of you can sit down to talk about your problems. At the conference, have your textbooks, notebooks, and assignments with you. Your teacher may need to look at them in order to help you.

When you talk with your teacher, you will probably also discuss your study schedule. Your teacher may want to know how you use your time in school and how much time you spend on your studies at home or in the library. Be honest in your answers. Your teacher can help you adjust your study schedule while helping you understand any areas in a subject that you find confusing. For example, your math teacher could explain to you what numerators and denominators are and how to find the least common denominator. This same teacher can also give you hints about special ways in which you can study efficiently and effectively for math class both at school and at home.

## Your Teacher as Counselor

Students usually have problems related to school. But they also have problems outside of school. They look for advice on how to deal with both kinds of problems. Your teachers are people you can turn to for such advice. To do so, you must have confidence in them. You must trust them and respect them.

*You should get to know your teachers. Most teachers want to know their students.*

You should get to know your teachers. Most teachers want to know their students. The time and effort will be well spent and rewarding. You want your teacher to be able to attach a personality to your name and to have some idea of who you are as a person. Teachers are normally delighted to find students who are willing and anxious to serve as active partners in their own education.

To get the most out of your education, you must have teachers with whom you can get along. Getting along with each other depends on you as much as it does on the teacher. Here are some suggestions about ways you can improve your relationships with your teachers:

1.  Be friendly. Begin your class and your work with each teacher by having a friendly attitude. Also, do not be deceived by appearances. Sometimes people are not what they appear to be. A sour-faced teacher may really be a friendly person underneath. And all teachers prefer a pleasant, smiling student to a disagreeable one with a permanent frown and rude manners.

2.  Be open-minded. Rumors about teachers are always circulating in every school. These rumors are often untrue. Try to be fair. Give each teacher a chance before you make up your mind about him or her.

3.  Ask for help. Teachers really do know a great deal more than you think about what is happening in their classes. They often know which students need help. Yet with so many students in a class, they may never offer help unless you show that you want it.

4.  Talk to your teachers. Talk to them about what is happening at school and in the world. Talk to them about their interests. Check with them about how your work is going from time to time, even when you think you are doing well. Communication between you and your teachers lets you understand each other better so that when problems come up, you can really talk to each other.

5.  Remember that teachers also have feelings. At different times, teachers may be happy, angry, or sad. Learn to tell the difference, and try to avoid communicating with teachers when the mood isn't right.

## Talk with Your Counselor

Sometimes, your teacher may not be the right person to help you with a problem. You may not feel comfortable talking to your teacher, especially if it is about a very personal problem or even a problem you have with that teacher. The person to talk to in such situations is your counselor. Counselors can do far more than help you decide on your course schedule. They are also trained to give advice on personal problems. And they keep everything you say to them confidential. They don't tell teachers what you have said.

Emotional upsets are a normal part of growing up. Unfortunately, they can seriously disrupt your studies at times. Don't make the mistake of trying to handle serious problems by yourself. Instead, talk to your counselor. If you are too shy to talk to your counselor about a problem, it is possible that there will be pamphlets in the counseling office that you may find helpful. Don't try to go it alone. Seek help when you feel you need it.

## Talk with the Librarian

Libraries are full of information that you need for papers, reports, and speeches, and you may be quite skilled at finding things in the library. However, it is frequently a good idea to tell librarians what you are researching and ask if they know any additional sources that you should see. Rarely will you be assigned a topic for which there is absolutely no information at a public library. Should this happen to you, the librarian can probably obtain the needed material from another library or get permission for you to use a special research library that contains the material.

If you have searched without any luck through every reference book in your home for some bit of important information, you can call your local library and the librarian will probably find you the answer or tell you how to find it. Central libraries in big cities usually have several librarians answering questions over the phone all day long. Even smaller libraries may have librarians who have the time to research phone questions. Look on your school and local librarians as your friends. They can help you solve many of your study and research problems.

*Look on your school and local librarians as your friends. They can help you solve many of your study and research problems.*

## Get a Tutor

Did you miss a few weeks of school last month and fall hopelessly behind in geometry? Perhaps you have never understood how to master verb conjugation in French. Or maybe you have moved into a school district where you are unfamiliar with the method of instruction and you find it difficult to keep pace with your fellow students. When you are up against the wall in one subject or all your schoolwork, and you need more help than a teacher or your family can be expected to give you, it's time to find a tutor.

The first place you should look for a tutor is at your school. Your teacher or counselor may be able to recommend one that is especially qualified to give you the help you need. Most schools also have a list of tutors who are willing to help students. Many of these people are teachers. Since tutoring can be expensive, you may wish to use a student tutor. Student tutors are usually members of service or scholarship organizations. Tutors can help you get back on the track quickly, so don't be afraid to seek their help.

## Other Helpers

Nearly every community has many people and organizations that are willing to help you study and learn your schoolwork. Within the last few years, learning centers have opened in most major cities. At these places, you can be helped with reading, math, and almost every other subject. You can also find help to prepare for special tests like the S.A.T. Look in the yellow pages of your phone book to see if there are learning centers in your community.

Don't forget to investigate what other help is available at your own school. Special courses on how to study may be offered during the school year at many schools. There is also summer school if you need to improve your skills in certain subject areas or have failed to pass a class.

Do not overlook the remedial classes, usually offered in reading and math, and the classes in study techniques that many colleges and universities offer through their extensions and schools of continuing education. More help is available at bookstores where you can find self-help books to improve skills such as note taking, learning vocabulary, and doing basic arithmetic. Also find out if your community has a hot line that you can call if you need immediate help while you are doing your homework.

*If you don't find the help that you need at first, keep looking—it is there.*

If you don't find the help that you need at first, keep looking—it is there. Just talk to your teachers and counselors until you find the help that you need.

Finally, when you look for help with your studies, don't forget your family. A mother who studied chemistry and calculus may be just the person to help you with science and math. And a father who is a lawyer may be able to help with social studies and business classes. Ask older brothers and sisters for help, also. They may have taken a course that is giving you problems, and they might be able to pass on some secrets for mastering it.

## Help Yourself

It's always a good idea to talk to teachers, counselors, and family about your study problems. But you need to take full control of your own study practices. This book has shown you where, when, and how to study. Ask yourself if you are doing what you must in order to study efficiently and effectively. Consider the suggestions given in this book. Are you currently using these suggestions? If not, try them out. They have worked for many students, and they will work for you if you give them a fair chance.

Keep in mind that you are not the only one who has problems with schoolwork. There are other students who also have problems, and they are just as worried as you are. But if you are willing to ask for help and to make an honest effort to do better, you can improve your schoolwork, learn more, and be more satisfied with yourself as a student and a person.

# Index